D0108217

THE SIX ARCHETYPES OF LOVE

"In *Stories We Need to Know*, Dr. Allan Hunter revealed six major archetypes that are active in each of us. Now, in his brilliant follow-up, *The Six Archetypes of Love*, Hunter shows us how these archetypes manifest in our love lives and how — for those who utilize the vital knowledge tl
far away."
—Dr. Pat Baccili, award-winning host
Thrive By! ™

The Urbana Free Library

To renew materials call
217-367-4057

"With enormous depth of knowledge and clear insight into the human psyche, Hunter's *The Six Archetypes of Love* reveals six essential profiles of the individual in love. Everyone wants love, reading Hunter's book is a first step to understanding it and, most importantly, making it happen."
—Sandra Sedgbeer, Editor in Chief, PlanetLightworker Magazine,
www.PlanetLightworker.com

Praise

"By exploring 3,000 years
archetypes that traditionall
generation. Western societ
formative power of myth;
the classics using archetyp
he read Dr. Hunter's work.
—Rahasya Poe, Lotus Guic

INITIATIVE

Findhorn Press is committed to preserving ancient forests and natural resources. We elected to print this title on 30% post consumer recycled paper, processed chlorine free. As a result, for this printing, we have saved:

7 Trees (40' tall and 6-8" diameter)
2,613 Gallons of Wastewater
5 million BTU's of Total Energy
336 Pounds of Solid Waste
630 Pounds of Greenhouse Gases

Findhorn Press made this paper choice because our printer, Thomson-Shore, Inc., is a member of Green Press Initiative, a nonprofit program dedicated to supporting authors, publishers, and suppliers in their efforts to reduce their use of fiber obtained from endangered forests.

For more information, visit www.greenpressinitiative.org

Environmental impact estimates were made using the Environmental Defense Paper Calculator. For more information visit: www.papercalculator.org.

THE SIX ARCHETYPES OF LOVE

From Orphan to Magician

Allan G. Hunter

FINDHORN PRESS

11-08
15-

First published by Findhorn Press 2008

ISBN: 978-1-84409-142-3

Edited by Jane Engel
Cover design by Lisa Ferdinandsen
Layout by e-BookServices.com
Printed and bound in America

1 2 3 4 5 6 7 8 9 10 11 12 13 14 13 12 11 09 08

Published by
Findhorn Press
305A The Park,
Findhorn, Forres
Scotland IV36 3TE

Tel +44(0)1309 690582
Fax +44(0)1309 690036
eMail info@findhornpress.com
www.findhornpress.com

Acknowledgements

My gratitude is deep and far ranging, so I'll attempt to list everyone and include those who probably don't know how much they've helped me.

I was fortunate to be granted a sabbatical from Curry College for the completion of this book. My gratitude to the President, Ken Quigley, and the Trustees is immense. I am also most grateful to Dean Sue Pennini who supported me in this endeavor and who agreed to release money from the Dean's Fund for the plates that appear in this book.

Material assistance in research was made possible by The Seth Sprague Educational and Charitable Foundation, and I am as always most grateful to Mrs. Arline Greenleaf and Mrs. Rebecca Greenleaf-Clapp for their belief in my work and the work of the Honors Program at Curry College. Without their support it is very doubtful that any of this would have been written. My research was helped in vital ways by the staff at Curry College Library, and particularly by Dr. Hedi Ben Aicha, who was always ready and enthusiastic in exploring recondite areas of knowledge.

My supporters and cheering team were led by Dr Ronald Warners, whose discussions and comments were invaluable, and who encouraged me to refine my ideas at meetings of BACAPT. Without his input no writing would have taken place. Professor Tom Shippey also loaned me more strength than perhaps he realizes.

Robert Atwan and Suzanne Strempek Shea were the perfect tactful advisors on so many topics during the writing process, and I am eternally grateful to them, and Greg Atwan's expertise in Greek drama and with *Antigone* in particular was much appreciated. Wisdom was also added by Linda Blackbourn, Vivian Brock, Jeffrey Di Iuglio, Dr. Martha Grace Duncan, Marlena Erdos, Kelly Ferry, Dorothy Fleming, Joan Elizabeth Goodman and Keith Goldsmith, Jeanette de Jong, Rea Killeen, Rick Klaich, Nora Klaver, Dr. Bessel van der Kolk, Douglas Kornfeld and Susan Lax, Sensei Koei Kuahara, Rebecca McClanahan, Jean Mudge, Jane Deering O'Connor, Iris Simmons MBE, Suzette Martinez Standring, Julie Stiles,

Cheryl Suchors, and Dennis Watlington. To David Whitley and to Andrew Peer-less, who have stood by me all these years as good friends and colleagues despite the intervening Atlantic Ocean, deep thanks.

Mary Lou Shields more than merits a specific mention as she gave me the periodic nudges that made all the difference, and kept me on my toes.

Thierry Bogliolo deserves special thanks for his continuing belief in this project, and for arranging for me to have the finest publicist in the world, Gail Torr. Many thanks also go to my editor, Jane Engel, for her patience and skill.

Others who contributed more than they know include Monique and Martin Lowe, Dr. Susan Peterson, Nick Portnoy, Anna Portnoy (who did a stellar job translating my handwriting into typescript), Bev Snow and the good people at the Watertown Center for the Arts, Paula Ogier and the staff of the Cambridge Center for Adult Education, Talbot Lovering and Tina Forbes, and Sally Young.

Gratitude and thanks also go to my mother, Elsa Hunter, who taught me the most important life lessons, and to my brother Donald, whose practical wisdom and unfailing good humor are always so reassuring

The deepest debt goes to Cathy Bennett, who has been the finest critic, advisor, support, and inspiration I could ever have hoped for. Gratitude is too weak a word to use.

Once again my most extensive debt is to all my students, who are, and always have been, my greatest teachers.

Table of Contents

Chapter One

Gauguin's Great Canvas

୨୨

Are we here in order to achieve things?
Or are we here in order to learn?

One of the most moving pieces of art I have ever seen is the enormous three part canvas painted by Gauguin, in Tahiti, on which he wrote the words, 'Where do we come from? What are we? Where are we going?' These questions have now become the painting's official title. The figures on the canvas don't seem especially to be contemplating these questions as they set about their various tasks. Perhaps that is the whole point. We live, we work, we pray (or we don't pray) we sit, we dream, just as the figures on the canvas are doing and these questions remain part of who we are. The questions are not there to make us panic and scramble for answers. None of the figures Gauguin painted seems desperate.

The questions are worth asking, though. Of course, questions like these may just be constructs that we human beings make for ourselves. There may be no important questions to ask, let alone answer. We have no concrete evidence to say that it's important for us even to address such ideas. Yet somehow we *feel* it to be important, even in a paradise like Tahiti. We seem to return to this idea that we do have a purpose and a goal. If this is true, then we must attempt to think about our lives in those terms and find an answer that works for us. We seem to need to make meaning in our lives. Perhaps this sounds like a vain pastime, so I'd point out merely that those who fail to find meaning are those who are most heavily represented in the ranks of the chronically depressed, the substance abusers, the incarcerated, and the suicidal.

Gauguin felt these questions keenly, and knew he'd created something un-usual in this extraordinary three-part, twelve foot wide painting he thought of as his 'dream'. He felt the canvas was the greatest thing he'd done, 'a philosophical work...comparable to the Gospels,' as he wrote. Later the same year he tried to kill himself, not out of despair but because he was convinced he had completed his life's work.

We may be here on earth for many reasons: to be successful; to be happy; to be good or virtuous; to create a beautiful painting. The list could go on forever. Some answers may seem more worthy than others. I personally find it hard to believe that humans are alive simply in order to gather dollar bills for their own pleasure, for example, or to be in control of cruel and repressive governments, or to use the media to manipulate unsuspecting populations into a state of misery. Most people would agree that these do not seem to be worthy goals for a career, let alone a lifetime, yet they don't seem to have diminished in popularity.

If we are on earth to ask questions, if we are here in order to learn from the experience of being human, then we have to ask what it is we are supposed to be learning.

Perhaps a possible answer lies in what we can witness whenever we see a new-born and its mother. For when we see them, whether in an under-funded hospital in Mumbai or enshrined as a Madonna and Child at the Vatican, we are aware of just one thing: the huge and incomprehensible strength of human love. The mother does not see only the trials ahead for her child or herself, although she may be aware that the world is cruel. But no matter how difficult the mother's situation she will love her child – even if she's forced to give it up for adoption later. That primary loving attachment is observable anywhere. The child craves love, if only in order to survive. Yet the desire to have a loving connection to others is very strong throughout our lives. Could it be that the very first lessons we learn as infants, the lessons of attachment, acceptance, and love, are in fact the ones we need most to explore in the rest of our lives?

So how important is that early love? Psychology and medical science have shown us that children who do not feel loved do not thrive. They tend to be underweight, less confident, and socially less well-adjusted. Their intelligence levels may also be affected. These are all statistically measurable. But there is more to consider. If we are given a firm grounding in love and in being cared for as infants, we develop the confidence to explore our world. In fact love tends to allow us to grow our courage, and so we look around and learn about how things work first within the safety of the family, then in the wider context of the community, and eventually in the seemingly endless confusions of the world. An ever-expanding series of possibilities awaits us as we grow.

We learn in the family to love those who are sometimes very different from ourselves, as well as how to love those who are just like us. In grade school we learn we have to respect everyone, which is another form of love, even if those people are sometimes our rivals or our enemies. And those challenges don't end in the classroom. When we leave school we find a bewildering world in which everyone has at least to try and get along, and where we look for a loving partner with whom to build our lives. We'll look for friends and for lovers fully aware that some people out there want to hurt us. We may also find ourselves engaging in the search for spiritual enlightenment or a closer communion with God. Some versions of God seem to lead towards destruction and anger. Others are more obviously loving. How will we choose? And how will we deal with those people whose belief systems are repugnant to us?

It seems as though this marvelous world of ours could be a vast, constantly developing opportunity for us to find out how to love each other – even under the most trying of circumstances. If we fail to love each other, accept each other, and respect differences we can be sure that peace will never occur, and at the heart of this is the need to accept ourselves.

If this is so then we are all, whether we like it or not, invited on this journey of exploration to find out about love.

Along the way we'll discover some interesting things. We'll see that there are six different levels of love – these are the six archetypes of the title – and we'll see that these exist in our literature, our art, our folk tales, and even in such places as the Tarot pack. We'll also see that as we move from stage to stage we retain the lessons and insights of the previous archetype, and we'll learn techniques so we can activate that energy whenever we need to access its benefits.

Notes

1. Gauguin's painting hangs in the Museum of Fine Arts, Boston. His reference to it as 'my dream' is from his letter of March 1899 to Andre Fontainas, quoted by Robert Goldwater in *Gauguin* (New York: Abrams, 1983), p. 114.

2. Gauguin refers to the painting as being 'comparable to the Gospels' in a letter to Daniel de Monfreid, Feb. 1898, quoted in Goldwater, *op. cit.*, p.110.

Chapter Two

The Journey to Love

Ꙩ

Why do so many of us get it wrong?
Historical backgrounds

Love is one of the most misunderstood concepts in our culture – in any culture. Turn on the radio and you'll get love songs. Even though Sting may sing about Sacred Love, and Steve Winwood may greet us with his plea to 'Bring me a higher love,' do we have any idea what these concepts actually mean? If we watch TV, the chances are we'll see the latest series which is all too often about people who can't manage to find meaningful relationships. *Sex and the City* was a smash hit, predicated on people not being happy in love but longing for it and finding sex instead. Even our most familiar way of describing love – *falling in love* – suggests that we're somehow up-ended and helpless when it happens.

In contrast to this, the much-repeated formula that half of all marriages in the USA end in divorce speaks to the failures of what some people consider to be love. It's a statistic that is eloquent of disappointment, yet also of the hope, the optimism that sends so many of us into a situation that has such a poor survival rate. We wouldn't choose a career that offered us a 50% chance of being out of work in a few years, and we wouldn't join an army that wounded its soldiers at that rate either. Yet weddings show no signs of dying out. And what of the myriads of people who live together?

There are all kinds of love, of course, and sexual love between two people is not the whole story, yet it does seem to be the point where the majority of people fail so spectacularly. If we can look at this as a part of a larger picture we can begin to make progress in understanding what love might be – what it might demand – in all its various forms. The longing for love is everywhere, clearly. The ability to understand it sufficiently to make it work is what's lacking. And that is why I am writing these pages.

I've been married, divorced, and am now happily married, so in some ways I write this with the mud of front-line trenches still on my boots. What wisdom I may have was earned, won the hard way, by making lots of mistakes and attempting to learn from them. I was tempted to give up my search – many times. But what I noticed is that even those who seem to have given up hope still long for some sort of attachment. We yearn for love, most of us. We flock to romantic Hollywood stories about it. We seem to require happy endings to our movies, sitcoms, and light reading. So why is it that for all our wishes that love should work out successfully, we are so poor at putting this desire into action?

I'd suggest it's because we have lost sight of what love is and how it works, and this happened many decades ago. In these pages I'll spell out that there is another way to understand what love is, and it depends upon us seeing that love exists at several distinct levels. As we grow in our lives we are invited to move through six stages – archetypal stages of personal and spiritual development. When we grow through these stages our definition of what love can be changes and deepens, and we see it anew. Seeing our lives in this way demands more from us. That's one reason that some people just don't seem to have a clue as to what love is – they may be stuck at a level that is not very advanced, and their confusions seem almost impossible to untangle. For the most part, people do not know that there are six stages, so how can they hope to get any clarity?

If we look at what our highest rated TV serials have to tell us about love, we'd have to say that the messages we get from them are confusing. Think of *Sex and the City* or *Desperate Housewives*; there is a huge amount of sex going on, and plenty of longing for love and lusting after tanned bodies, yet we'd be hard pressed to say that there is much loving behavior in all that plotting, conniving, and backstabbing. The characters in *Desperate Housewives* are certainly attractive, and we may enjoy watching the situations they get themselves into, yet they are, well, *desperate.* It looks like they're scrambling for love but have no real sense what that might mean. But before we write off this wildly energetic and entertaining series we have to notice that one of the more interesting parts about this show is the way it is narrated. Starting with the first series we have voice-overs by characters who are dead (primarily Mary Alice Young, and then Rex Van De Kamp at one point), who are looking into their neighbors' lives with a more detached sense than any of the living characters. In fact this trick of narrational presentation seems to ask us in the audience to observe the frantic actions with a certain coolness, as we reflect on the confusions that so many of the characters seem to fall into. The series seems to know that there is more to life than most of the individual characters can grasp. Aside from making general comments on the situations we are watching, the deceased Mary Alice Young doesn't tell us what that *more* is.

If we're to understand how we as a culture became so confused, we may have to look back to see how love has been depicted through the ages.

The Historical Background

Part of the problem is the word "love" itself. It's a notoriously slippery concept that is routinely used as a blanket term. We love our friends, our parents (well, mostly), our children, our spouses, our work, our home team, our job, chocolate torte … At least the ancient Greeks had more than one word for love; they differentiated between love of friends, love of home, greed, and erotic love. The Greeks were splendid category makers.

They also ran their lives in ways we'd find confusing. So it was accepted for a man to have homosexual relations with young boys (upon which he might, or might not, act), take pleasure with a prostitute/mistress (again, he might not act on his sexual impulses), and also be respectful to a wife who was to bear his children, whom he was expected to educate and train appropriately – and perhaps even to love. Such a flexible arrangement was considered entirely within the normal, and seems to have covered most of the sexual variants available to men, more or less. Today we'd find this unacceptable and probably conclude that the Greeks were sex-obsessed. And that would be a really excellent way to ignore the deep wisdom that they were capable of, even though the way they lived their lives doesn't suit our imagined proprieties.

A little later in history we see the Romans, like the Greeks, differentiating between erotic love and mere sexual greed, yet their plays, and especially their comedies, seem to prefer to ridicule the lover. A man in love was a man who was no longer reasonable and therefore no longer truly a man. Virtue, a concept invented by the Romans, is a word derived from *vir*, meaning a man. Manliness was the same thing as Virtue to them, and had everything to do with getting ahead. It didn't have much to do with a tender appreciation of a sexual partner.

The Romans certainly were interested in sexual desire, though. Standing midway between the Romans and the Greeks the poet Ovid (who died in A.D.17) responded to the Roman world's enthusiasm for various sexual themes by retelling myths that were essentially Greek, and these stories were cherished in the centuries that followed. Yet there is one over-riding factor in these tales and especially in his *Metamorphoses*: lovers are changed into less-than-human form by their lusts, or while trying to evade other people's lusts. Sexual promptings were felt, therefore, to be somehow destructive. They turned humans into animals or plants. Daphne is transformed into a laurel bush rather than give in to Apollo; Syrinx becomes a reed to avoid Pan; and Philomela, violated, becomes a nightingale. Even the gods were turned into animals by lust. Jove becomes a bull to carry off Europa, and a swan to make love to Leda. In fact the disgraceful antics of the Olympian gods, all sleeping with each other and betraying each other, are hardly a model of behavior. The anarchic nature of sexual desire is well portrayed; but *love*?

At first glance we could be forgiven if we were to think the ancients were hopelessly confused. Yet that would be to miss the point. The Greeks were interested in depicting love in *all* its forms, which suggests that it was a topic of continuing fascination and importance for them and that they had a sophisticated awareness of the issue. The legends of the gods and goddesses can be seen as examples of how poorly people will behave at times when they think they are in love – even though the examples are extreme. In case we doubt this we have only to look at the very familiar example of Narcissus. In the legend Narcissus is a beautiful youth of 16 who rejects all lovers including Echo, a nymph who loves him and is eager to seduce him. Echo has already been sentenced by Juno to repeat only the words of others because she would habitually do that to delay Juno and prevent her uncovering Jove's adulteries. Echo, like a child caught trying to placate jealous warring parents, already knows about sex and deception, and has seen Juno love without having her affections fully returned. Interestingly, Echo fixes her attention on the one person who will scorn her, which is just what we'd expect given her earlier experiences.

One of the other rejected lovers prays that Narcissus will fall in love with himself so he will know what it is like to be hopelessly in love. And so, when Narcissus sees his own reflection in a pool of water he finds it so attractive that he gives up food and drink and eventually dies, pining for the youth in the reflection.

Delightful, we may say, because it explains echoes and why the narcissus flower likes to grow near water, over which its blooms hang, seeming to admire themselves. But obviously this is not all the legend conveys. Think of those young men and women who reach their teenage years and become fixated on how they look, spending hours in front of the mirror trying to be some idealized image of themselves they have got from a magazine or a movie. No one can tell them they're wasting their time, just as Echo couldn't tempt Narcissus back to reality and the warm love of a real person. Think of how many young people starve themselves because of self-image confusions, or perhaps they go to the other extreme with steroids that bulk them up. They are in love with a projection of their own self-image. They will also tend to have friends who look and dress as they do and perhaps at this point in their lives are not capable of true attachment to another because they are so self-involved. Those who do love them are forced to fit in with their self-involvement, like Echo, and must always agree with them. Isn't this what we see all too often with teenagers in cliques? Echo is surely mirrored in the tongue-tied teenager, dazzled by the one he or she pines for, yet also nursing a sense of hatred because she feels so rejected by those she longs to be fully accepted by. In one brief legend the Greeks were able to sum up with consummate elegance an entire life-situation that every young person will witness in some form, and that represents a real possibility for the psyche to be stunted. Narcissistic people are an actual problem today, still, since they cannot seem to see anything except their own world. For them it is always about *me*, and perhaps always will be. Consider Narcissus' fate if ever you have to deal with someone who seems to be a narcissist. Consider, as well, Echo's fate – which is what one may find oneself taking on if one has to deal with a narcissist. Another version of Echo appears in fixated individuals and stalkers, which is exactly what Echo seems to be in her attraction to and ultimate persecution of her love object. Narcissus, we'll recall, talks to his reflection and Echo is fated to repeat his last few words, which he thinks come from his reflection and this binds him tighter to his delusion. Unintentionally she adds to his torture. She cannot just leave as any sensible person would.

If we are to make sense of this we have to see this situation as one that could happen to any young person and see it as one in which he or she can take either role. If we know that this phase awaits the growing youngster we can alert him or her to it, be aware of what's happening, and help with the successful navigation of this passage – since it is a place where love can obviously be shipwrecked.

And in case we miss the point, the legend gives us one more detail. Narcissus' mother Liriope was a river nymph who was raped by the river god Cephisus. Rape is always an act of self-involvement on behalf of the rapist – a narcissistic power-trip, in fact – and the victim is always traumatized, left untrusting and suspicious. Narcissus, we recall, is a youth who is loved by everyone, men and women alike; but he rejects all advances, not just Echo's. He seems to be eager to avoid entanglements, especially those that his mother suffered from, and hence he rejects everyone. Whether we see the story of Echo and Narcissus as a myth about self involvement based in fear, as a story about rejection and fixation, or whether we choose to see it as what can happen to boys who are brought up by mistreated mothers, with the resultant crisis of sexual identity the child may then go through – well, that's up to us. It has all those elements.

Ovid recorded so many of these Greek myths because even though these legends were already old at the time he knew they had real power, and he strove to render them in all their richness because he recognized their enduring worth.

The point we need to take from this is that the Greeks clearly had a deep insight into the nature of love and they explored in their myths the things that no society ever manages to get quite right in the daily world. In our time we've forgotten how to understand the myths, and we tend to judge the Greeks and Romans by what they did rather than by how they thought. That's a bit like criticizing a man for driving in a horse and buggy when, in fact, he has a mind that can understand inter-planetary rocketry. So the considerable wisdom of Greek myths was buried for centuries. It's not that they didn't communicate good insights, it's that we forgot how to listen to their communications. The Greeks themselves had no trouble understanding their myths. That's why they kept repeating and recording them – because they knew there was wisdom in them, and because they worked.

Part of what we'll be doing in this book is looking at the confusions that history, myth, and literature have handed us about love and pointing out that the confusions are not necessarily within the stories themselves. In fact they may be of recent origin, based in cultural prejudices that have sprung up in our fast-moving, progress-obsessed times.

So let's take a moment to consider further how love may have become a difficult topic over the centuries, and why.

The words of St. Paul are not a bad place to start since to some extent they mirror our modern confusions about meaning. In his first epistle to the Corinthians, chapter 13, he wrote: "And now abideth faith, hope and love – and the greatest of these is love." The word 'love' is rendered as 'charity' in the King James Bible of 1611 – which is still the official version of the Protestant Bible – and this wording brought it close to the Latin word *caritas*. Since some versions of the text had been copied in Latin this made sense. However, it wasn't until about 250 years ago that the great preacher John Wesley questioned this etymology and insisted that *love* was the better word because it had no overtones of wealthy people giving sums of money to the deserving poor. *Caritas* had a meaning of loving kindness that just wasn't translating properly as Charity, and the concept of what divine love might be was consequently muddied for all. Wesley may have been inspired or plain wrong, but we can also venture that the Latin writers were trying to be clear that they were not talking about sexual love, for if they had been they would probably have used the word *amor*.

In fact, going back in time from Wesley, in early medieval European society the idea of sexual love was nothing if not confused. Love, when it struck, was often depicted as a disaster that threatened the all-important loyalties to the local lord and his clan. Anglo-Saxon poetry from *Beowulf* to King Arthur's legends is filled with the horrifying accounts of what happened when men fell in love with women who were someone else's property. Love tended to make them forget their loyalties to the king or the clan. That's what destroyed Arthur's Round Table. Lancelot and Queen Guinevere's adulterous affair broke the more usual bond of loyalty between king and subject – and civil war was the outcome. Love's power was acknowledged, but only in the anarchic, dangerous sense of sexual desires that could not be contained. Think of Abelard and Heloise struggling unsuccessfully against their longing for each other, or of Tristan and Iseult. In each case love is a disaster.

In *Beowulf* we have a sense that love is doomed to be destroyed by those over-powering tribal loyalties. For example, when the bard comes to sing to Beowulf and the others, the song he chooses is called *The Fight at Finnsburgh*. In that tale king Finn of the Frisians is married to Hildeburh of the Danes in a match that is supposed to bring peace. Unfortunately Finn's desire for revenge for old wrongs causes him to attack his brother-in-law Hnaef while he is a guest in his home and a full-scale battle erupts. Hildeburh doesn't know who to support, her husband or her brother. The next year the Danes return, kill her husband and drag her back to Denmark. It's hardly a happy end for her since she's lost relatives on both sides. It seems as if the demands of loyalty and loyalty's relentless partner – revenge – destroy love.

This is one of the very few references in *Beowulf* to the concept of love between a man and a woman. Beowulf himself has no romantic attachments – we never hear if he marries, although we can assume he would have done – and his energies are all taken up in being a loyal subject and finally an upright king.

The story of Tristan and Iseult shows a similar conflict to Hildeburh's. The tale went through many variations right up until the Nineteenth Century where it appears as Wagner's opera *Tristan und Isolde,* and the plot varies a little with each re-telling, but the major components carry the same message about love. It's a story that pre-dates Launcelot and Guinevere, and is one of the great, influential love tragedies of all time.

In the early legends King Mark of Cornwall sends his most trusted knight and relative, Tristan, to collect from Ireland the bride he has arranged to marry. Iseult, the young Irish princess, asks her mother what she will do if, when she meets her as yet unknown husband, he doesn't love her. Luckily her mother is a sorceress who gives her a flask full of a love potion to meet this situation head on (in some versions it is her maid Brangwayn who is put in charge of the potion). All seems well for the happiness of the wedding and the ultimate establishment of peace between warring kingdoms. But then fate takes a hand. Tristan and Iseult accidentally drink the potion. It works, just as it was supposed to, except on the wrong people. The young couple cannot resist its magic, and spend the rest of the story trying hard to overcome their longing, without success. Tristan is haunted by his treachery to his king and his friend; Iseult is tortured by her need to dissemble, and when whispers get out that all is not well, her family decides that the peace treaty she is supposed to be a part of can no longer be upheld, and they see her as a traitor also.

The first point that we may want to hold up here is that, to the recorders of the legend (whoever they were) and their audiences, love was dangerous because it could upset important political loyalties and ultimately resulted in betrayals, wars, and death. In addition this was clearly a tension that fascinated them, which is a pretty sure indication that the audience knew first hand how love and sexual desire could tempt anyone to want to run away from ties of family loyalty. They'd all felt it, or at least seen it, and they loved hearing about it. The third point – and it's an important one about perception – is that love is seen as something that comes from outside oneself, created by a potion or a spell, against which there is no remedy. Neither Tristan nor Iseult is morally weak in any way, no more than if they had both caught the flu.

Love that arrives from outside the self, as with Eros and his arrows shot from afar, makes us able to pity the afflicted lovers, but it doesn't give us a strong sense of what love is. In French there is still an interesting expression for this kind of sudden, overwhelming, love – *coup de foudre* – which is roughly translated as 'thunderstruck'. It's not a bad description of what can happen, but notice how helpless it renders the person who feels it.

The tale of Tristan and Iseult may not be new, but it shows no evidence of dying out. A new movie version appeared in 2006, (*Tristan and Isolde*) which fully mirrors this idea of the destructive power of love. The love triangle is a familiar theme (it takes us right back to *Desperate Housewives*) yet if we look back to the medieval period almost nowhere do we get a sense of the inspiring or regenerative powers that love most surely has. The sole exception to this was the Love of God, which as the centuries progressed became more and more linked with the suppression of sexuality, the tendency to treat oneself as a "miserable sinner" bound for hell unless one repented of every carnal thought, and a general feeling that the world was a wicked place of fleshly temptations, where everyone was tainted by "original sin."

Not a pretty prospect.

Even though original sin was first seen as disobedience in the story of Adam and Eve, it evolved into an issue of disobedience based in sexual desire as the church explained it. The church, with its celibate clerics, feared sexual love and still does. Unfortunately this fear led to repressions that have come back to haunt us all in the form of the sexual abuse scandals involving priests and children and the devastation such abuse can cause in young lives.

In each of these examples drawn from literature we'll notice one constant, and it is that love is seen as a static concept. There is no attempt to show that love can grow or change; it can meet challenges ('for richer, for poorer…') but there is almost no exploration of the way love can deepen and develop, or fail to grow and so wither and die. One is either in love or not.

Even Chaucer's great love poem *Troilus and Criseyde* has the Trojan lovers forced apart by circumstances beyond their control. When Criseyde has to take her place in a trade of captives with the Greeks she all too soon agrees to become Diomede's lover. Troilus' despair turns him into a spirited and reckless fighter, but when he is killed and floats up to the eighth sphere of heaven Chaucer asks us to reflect upon how insignificant sexual love and attraction really are. It may be a sentiment in tune with religious orthodoxy, but it leaves us feeling somewhat flat.

But wait: our modern sensibilities may lead us astray here, since Chaucer gives us a detailed description of Troilus' love – his longing, his need for secrecy, his devotion, his despair in the face of betrayal – and then contrasts it with an entirely different perspective as Troilus ascends to heaven. Rising above it all he looks down with a critical eye, and provides us with the opportunity to question all we have observed.

But Chaucer does far more than this. From the start of the poem he reverses the cliché of the poor young maid seduced and abandoned, because it is royal Troilus who is the inexperienced, fainting, virginal lover, and Criseyde who is the more experienced widow. She is practical in guarding her reputation and status, rather than being wracked by moral questions because, after all, her father has defected to the enemy. So we are forced to see the situation as other than a stereotype of the knight and the maiden. Later writers such as Henryson and Dunbar returned to the tale to rewrite their own versions of it, and were less kind than Chaucer to Criseyde. In fact their works sometimes seem like the most callous forms of misogyny. Chaucer's view is very different since it seems to invite discussion about every aspect of the love affair we have seen described, and as it does so it shows us a society that was vitally engaged in trying to comprehend this troublesome feeling. Glib answers are always available for the close-minded. Chaucer's greatness is in refusing easy stereotyping. Chaucer, we must remember, was writing for the Court, where such discussions were welcomed. Much of the rest of the population had no leisure for this type of fine speculation.

This split is never more evident than in the medieval confusions over the conventions of courtly love. Briefly put, this was a response to the arranged marriages of the time, which were all about property. Where there is marriage without love there will be love without marriage, and so courts throughout Europe found themselves adopting a code in which it was quite acceptable for a knight to be pledged to a lady, even a married lady, as her 'lover,' provided they did not slip into adultery. He would be loyal to her, raise her to the level of a goddess, and even die defending her name – and preferably do so while never revealing his feelings publicly.

What this signals to us is that in bygone eras people were fully aware of the power of sexual love and the need to idealize the loved one, yet they had very little idea as to what to do with this urge, nor how to align it with religion. Religion insisted that only the love of God mattered – but that is, I feel, a failure of the religious establishment's vision rather than a failure of the wisdom we can observe in the literature. So literature was energetic in *depicting* the tensions of the age – but had no solutions to offer which did not go against the received dogma.

With this in mind let's look again at the hugely popular legend of Tristan and Isolde. The storytellers are very specific about Tristan's brotherly love for King Mark, as well as his loyalty to him as his king, and to his people. They show three different aspects of love and loyalty right there. Then the tale tests that loyalty to breaking point by bringing in Isolde. Isolde herself has a loyal and loving sense of duty to her father, who is her king, her mother, and her kinsfolk. Both Tristan and Isolde desire peace between the kingdoms and to some extent wish to be selfless idealists. When they fall in love they experience the full strength of their emotions and know that this kind of situation cannot be made 'right' no matter how much they love each other. They don't have the option of resigning as some of our politicians do, to "spend more time with the family". The story is, therefore, a careful examination of a rather perplexing problem and shows considerable sophistication about the forces of love, even if it offers no easy answers. This is why it's important to bring in Chaucer's *Troilus* because that poem continues the discussion beyond death. Troilus, as he rises to heaven is able to reflect that there is a higher love that he never even considered before, and that his sorrow was caused to a great extent by his refusal to see this larger picture, in which he would have to ask what love is *at the highest level*. It's the equivalent of the *Desperate Housewives* voice-overs we noted earlier, except we're left in no doubt as to how he could be thinking about the whole situation. It's not until that point that Troilus begins to wonder what it was he was supposed to learn from all this.

This is a question that echoes through Shakespeare's plays, too. The doomed love of Romeo and Juliet is exactly comparable to Chaucer's earlier poem and, when the two lovers lie dead on the stage and Montague and Capulet vow to make peace, we would be remiss if we didn't notice that Friar Lawrence's desire to heal the rift between the two houses has finally come to pass, but at a terrible cost. The higher love – peace, brotherly forgiveness, and understanding – is achieved only when sexual love has been transcended. The Prince puts it beautifully when in almost the last lines of the play he says: "Go hence, to have more talk of these sad things" (v.iii.306). He is explicitly *ordering* both Montague and Capulet to go and talk together so that they and their households can learn about the various levels and meanings of love – since peace cannot be maintained without this understanding and openness. This surely is a reflection of what the audience would do. They would respond to the drama and they would mull the experience over, afterwards. This is what Aristotle expected the audience of a play to do, as he makes clear in his description of Catharsis as an essential aspect of the successful drama. The play is an invitation to further thought.

Shakespeare's message has been lost in countless productions that have failed to consider that point fully. It seems plain that Shakespeare is pointing us to a far more complex discussion of love than just sexual attraction and its challenges (although that's pretty complex in itself) since Romeo and Juliet's complete absorption in each other is just one element. The play is much richer if we stop focusing on what we expect to see – a romantic love story – and observe its larger resonances as an exploration of many different kinds of love, loyalty and attachment. Think of the love the Nurse has for Juliet, and how she urges her to give up Romeo and accept Paris when things go awry. What sort of love is that? What sort of loyalty? What sort of love and loyalty does Friar Lawrence have for Romeo when he also wants to secure a peace between the two houses but is prepared to lie in order to do so? And he effectively abandons Juliet in the tomb, thus ensuring her suicide, which she could not have achieved if he'd stayed. Is that loving? According to Christian doctrine at the time her soul would have gone straight to hell. And what about that absurd 'loyalty' of each house for its own name and status that breeds so many fights? Whatever else Shakespeare is doing he's certainly asking questions about different types of love and attachment. These points have routinely been relegated to the background – which is a bit like going to a five course meal and focusing only on dessert.

In fact the warfare between the two houses only results in them hurting themselves. They both lose their only direct heirs and so they are effectively both extinct. Warfare is a way of hurting oneself, and therefore of not loving oneself. It's a lesson we'd do well to consider even today as we lose soldiers in our various wars.

Despite these searching questions the general tendency of the ordinary people in Shakespeare's time remained to tell their sons and daughters what to do and whom to marry. Love was not to derail wedding alliances if it could be avoided. Love was nice, but money ensured that no one would starve. Society may have had a rather grim and pragmatic approach to love, yet literature continued to dwell upon trying to understand it. Not surprisingly it depicted the ways that love was thwarted by materialistic concerns – since that was what one saw almost everywhere.

Real insight and wisdom is undeniably present in these tales but, in each of the cases we've looked at, we have seen how the dictates of a materialistic society have interfered. It's as if people were aware of what love could be but they really wanted it to be something else, something that wouldn't get in the way of business, money, property, and basic survival.

In the Eighteenth and Nineteenth centuries we can detect a move to redress the imbalance. Women novelists began to make a case for love matches rather than marriages of an arranged sort, and very often we are delighted to see that characters take a long time to recognize that they are in love – and so learn a lot about themselves in the process. Jane Austen surprised her readers by having Elizabeth Bennet refuse to marry a clergyman she did not love – she holds out for real happiness and wins the much more sensible Mr. Darcy, who also happens to be rich. It is through the works of Austen, George Eliot, the Brontë sisters and others, that the idea of love between a man and a woman that could be nurturing and productive was revealed, gradually. It took nearly a century of writers, some of the greatest of whom were women.

Jane Austen may be the most influential of writers on this topic. We have only to think of Elizabeth Bennet's dawning recognition that she and Darcy are made for each other, or to consider Emma Woodhouse's shock at coming to see that she loves Mr. Knightley and can marry no one else, to know that love is being treated with a more exploratory sense than before. Love is seen to grow within the characters over time. Jane Austen herself contrasts these examples, comically, when she has Harriet Smith fall in love with three men in quick succession, and has Lydia Bennet fall in love with anything in a uniform – the only warning being that someone has caught her eye. It's against such shallowness that Jane Austen fought, and in the process she was plowing new and fertile soil when she wrote about how we can grow to love others over time. For the first time love was seen as a dynamic force.

And so, to some extent, that has led us to where we are now.

The slight difficulty about the change in attitudes fostered by the Nineteenth century is that it is still a limited view. For example, each story by Jane Austen tends to end with the marriage of the happy pair. We don't get much of a sense of how they are likely to arrange their lives afterwards. Presumably children and the duties required of her as Mr. Knightley's wife will keep Emma busy for a lifetime, and she is but one representative of the ideally "sensible" marriage that we are expected to approve of. Yet in our age there is far more than this to look forward to. If one marries at twenty-one – as many Austen heroines seem to – nowadays we can expect to live some sixty years after that. Recent literature doesn't say much about this, which is partly why we have lost our way.

For centuries literature was a rich source of instructional information about how to live, within the parameters of its specific time period. Each age had its particular blind spots, yet if we can look beneath the surface of these tales we will see that there is considerable wisdom about love and our longing for it and its centrality in our life journey. We could compare this situation to the growth of a tree. It grows from a seedling and will be a tree, no matter what. A gardener may decide to come along and prune it according to the fashion of the times, and create a topiary statue of whatever catches his fancy. Yet it's still a tree no matter how its outward shape may have been trimmed. If we look for the real essence of the literature, for those inner structures that are like the trunk and branches of the tree, we will be able to see that writers have been telling us about the nature of love for centuries, but we have to know what to look for and then read the books that can help us most. The problem is that we're not reading them. We're watching soaps (and that's an interesting version of life!) or reading Bridget Jones or watching Hollywood movies that are highly financed but not, sadly enough, in touch with any deep wisdom about how to live or how to love.

If we wish to learn more about love we may have to think about it in a different way. By choosing to consider it in terms of archetypes we can find a more productive way forward. For Shakespeare and Austen certainly see love as being different for characters who are at different levels of awareness, and each of these levels corresponds to an archetype, of which there are six.

The Six Archetypes

In my book *Stories We Need to Know* I showed how literature – and by implication the human mind – seems to express its sense of human development in terms of six specific stages. These are presented in the form of six archetypal figures, which have appeared throughout Western literature from the earliest times. These archetypes appear always in the same form, always in the same order, in all of the works recognized as great literature in the Western Canon.

If this is true – and it was the purpose of that book to show that it is true – then we can use these six stages to consider what is possibly this most complex of human aspirations; the longing for love. As a person grows through the six stages so does her awareness of what love might be, and what this unruly emotion may demand. It is quite accurate to say, then, that the concept of love cannot be defined or even properly illustrated without referring to how we experience it at different points in our lives. An acorn, a seedling, and a full grown oak tree are all essentially the same creature, but entirely different in their levels of development. It would be absurd to pretend that they are exactly the same thing. Love is no different and has to be treated accordingly.

Notes

1. Sting. *Sacred Love*, 2003.
2. Winwood, Steve. *Higher Love*, 1986.
3. *Sex and the City* ran on HBO from 1998 until 2004 for a total of six seasons. It

won several Emmys and other prizes. A movie is scheduled for mid-2008. The series is currently in re-runs and on DVD. Its appeal has not faded as yet.

4. *Desperate Housewives* first aired on ABC in 2004. It has won multiple Emmy, Golden Globe, and Screen Actors Guild awards. In April 2007 it was reported to be the most popular show in its demographic worldwide with an estimated audience of 115 to 119 million (wikipedia).

5. Ovid, *Metamorphoses*, trans. Rolfe Humphries (Bloomington: Indiana Univ. Press, 1955, 1983). Ovid finished *Metamorphoses* in 8 AD.

6. The story of Narcissus and Echo is in Book III of the *Metamorphoses*, lines 438-505, in Humphries' edition, pp.67-73.

7. St Paul, 1 Corinthians 13. The Wesley translation is to be found at http://wesley.nnu.edu/john_wesley/wesley_NT/07-1cor.html

8. *Beowulf: A New Verse Translation,* trans. Seamus Heaney (New York: Norton, 2001).

9. *The Letters of Abelard and Heloise,* trans. Peter Abelard (London: Penguin, 1998).

10. *The Romance of Tristan and Iseult* exists in many versions. I have used the edition adapted by J. Butler, and translated by Hilaire Belloc (London: Dover Editions, 2005). The earliest version of the story may have been by Chrétien de Troyes in 1170. This version was probably incorporated into Sir Thomas Malory's *Le Morte D'Arthur* (*c.* 1469). A readily available translation of Malory, edited by R. M. Lumiansky, was published by Scribners in 1982.

11. *Tristan and Isolde.* The movie was released in 2006, Executive Producer Ridley Scott. It starred James Franco and Sophia Myles.

12. The Fall of Man is told in *Genesis*, Chapter 3.

13. *Troilus and Criseyde.* The best text is in *The Complete Works of Geoffrey Chaucer,* ed. F. N. Robinson (Oxford: Oxford University Press, 1970).

14. Robert Henryson lived from c. 1424 until c. 1506. *The Testament of Cresseid* was for many years considered a continuation of Chaucer's original poem. See Robert Henryson, *Poems*, ed. Charles Elliot (Oxford: OUP, 1963). William Dunbar lived from c. 1456 until c.1513 and is considered to be a 'Scottish Chaucerian'. *The Tretis of the Tua Mariit Wemen and the Wedo* is the work in which he is uncharitable in his assessment of Criseyde and of women in general. It can be found in William Dunbar, *Selected Poems,* ed. Harriet Harvey-Wood (London: Routledge/Fyfield, 2003).

15. William Shakespeare, *The Complete Works*, ed. Peter Alexander (Collins, London, 1970). All Shakespeare quotations are from this volume.

16. Jane Austen, *Pride and Prejudice* (1813), and *Emma* (1816).

17. Helen Fielding, *Bridget Jones' Diary* (London: Picador, 1998).

Chapter Three

How the Six Archetypes Work

&

Love makes anything and everything worthwhile. Without love a mother is mere conscripted labor. Without love a father might be simply a stranger who appears after the workday is over. Take away love and marriage is just another financial arrangement. Without love siblings are merely murderous rivals, like Cain and Abel.

Understanding love is a bit like understanding gravity: we can pretend it isn't there and still function, but it takes noticing it and seeing how it works to be able to feel the full majesty of its power. The Wright brothers knew all about gravity – and how they could use it to their advantage to explore an entirely new dimension. And for a while, those who thought the brothers were impractical dreamers ridiculed them for their efforts.

It's time we, too, understood love a little better and to do that we need to understand the six archetypal stages of human development.

Stories We Need to Know showed that the six levels of spiritual development work as a series of archetypes. These are The Innocent, The Orphan, The Pilgrim, The Warrior-Lover, The Monarch, and The Magician.

We start as **Innocents,** as babies, as newcomers. We don't know the rules, but we do want to attach to others and trust them. This is what a baby does in successful mother-child relationships. The child learns how to feed and to cooperate while being fed, and extends total trust and love. In return the mother feels love that is commonly described as "unconditional." Mother doesn't care if the child is a little crotchety or homely, she loves it just the same, without reserve. Ask any parent of a disabled child, or one with Down's syndrome.

Unfortunately the complete trust the child has in the world is not a realistic stratagem to live with. Children are warned not to trust all adults, and especially not strangers with candy. All is not well in paradise. Parents are not perfect, and mother and father can't always make everything better. This recognition is the start of the **Orphan** phase.

The Orphan realizes that all is not perfect but agrees to attach to others anyway, for safety, and so she seeks to be 'adopted' by people she thinks are safe. In

Nick Hornby's novel *About a Boy*, Marcus is deeply frightened when his erratic mother tries to kill herself and so he resolutely sets about adopting and being adopted by as many friends as he can manage to secure. It's a delightful book and shows the Orphan at his twelve-year-old best. Safety, for Marcus, is in the number of people he can gather around him who are reliable supporters. As he works to introduce all the people in his life to each other he finds he is, unwittingly, getting them to care for each other, too. And love grows.

Adoption is fine for a while, of course, but everyone feels the urge to explore beyond themselves. We all have to leave school, leave our parents, leave home, or we can't find who we are when we are on our own. This can be frightening and some people can't manage it for very long. They scurry to the safety of the secure job, making sure they get themselves adopted by the group, the organization, or the expectations of those around them. They settle down and fit in. The Orphan has looked around, seen what the challenges are, and has decided to go back to being an Orphan.

Yet if we do venture beyond the conventional, and stay on that path, and if we do decide that it's worth seeking for something more, we can become **Pilgrims**. As Pilgrims we leave behind conventional comforts, we take to the road looking for meaning, which often means we go looking for the sense of purpose that we hope will come with love. The Hippie movement ("Make Love not War") was famous for pilgrimages of various sorts. The thousands who flocked to Woodstock, to Altamont, to all the open air concerts of the time – all of them were on some sort of search, whether they knew it or not. Perhaps they just wanted the experience, or the drugs, or the free sex. But they wanted something and they wanted it badly. So hippies traveled to Marrakesh, to Katmandu, to Cairo, to Yogis in India, to communes in Nevada, to surf beaches in Hawaii. On the way quite a few forgot what they were searching for and simply wandered around until, Orphans again, they found a home.

A few knew what they were looking for, and found it.

When they did so they made a claim that transformed them into people who had taken on a real cause. They became Warriors. And just as one cannot fight for something one does not love and respect, they became aware of love.

This stage, which we will call the **Warrior-Lover**, is when the individual commits to another person, or a cause, or sometimes both. This is the point at which the person who loves makes a real commitment to a relationship, and in a way that accepts the other person as one who will change and grow. This means that life will be a challenge sometimes, as each partner will have to understand the other person and the changes each of them goes through, and each will have to adapt accordingly. How different this is from the old paradigm of the man telling the woman who she was supposed to be.

Yet as we know, commitment and energy in a relationship are not always enough, and just as, for example, gifted teachers discover that they can be of more use passing on their knowledge to other teachers rather than teaching every class, so too the Warrior-Lover begins to want to nurture on a broader scale. Whether that means the energetic executive gets promoted to be a director of other executives, or perhaps it means mom teaching her kids how to do their own laundry and take care of themselves, the effect is the same. The hands-on Warrior-Lover begins to allow more space for others. Trust is born of that – and what love can flourish without trust? I give trust to another person; she respects that, enjoys the feeling of being trusted, and returns the compliment. When trust is established the Warrior-Lover ceases to be a one man or one woman army and becomes, instead, a **Monarch**.

Perhaps the easiest way to understand this transformation is that the Warrior-Lover tends to be committed to a special relationship with another, and at a certain point this relationship has to open to include a wider sense of what one can do with one's life. The Warrior-Lover might start in a strong loving relationship with a significant other and devote huge amounts of time and energy to that. There comes a time, though, when each person is going to want a wider acquaintance, a greater role within society. The loving duo, typically, might find that their children lead them into more connection with their neighbors and society, or with the local school system for example, and this awareness of new issues may prompt them to take on leadership roles within their newer, larger social circle. This is the point at which they can become Monarchs.

Monarchies are almost always paired, man and woman. This archetype is a symbolic representation of the fusion of the stereotypical 'male' executive power with the 'female' virtues of nurturing and compassion. This fusion must happen *within* each individual, just as ying and yang together make up a complete circle. To reach this level we have to know when to be strict and when to be compassionate. Just as the populace relies on the Monarch to do the correct thing for the whole kingdom, so too the Monarch has to be responsive to the needs of the people around him or her. When this contract of loving interdependency fails the Monarch will not last long. Just before the French Revolution Marie Antoinette's famous statement when told that the poor had no bread to eat was, "Let them eat cake." She simply couldn't imagine that anyone might be hungry because she never was, and she did not bother to make an effort to ascertain what was really going on in the kingdom. And so the French Revolution swept her and many others to the guillotine; tyranny, which is rule without love or compassion, seldom lasts long.

The Monarch's task is to get better and better at trusting, nurturing, instructing, guiding, and building love relationships. This love may well be extended to the idea of the state, or the Empire, or something similar but not in a blind, jingoistic way. It is a deeper love based not in wishing to be attached to something but rather in a profound sense of being *responsible* for that attachment. The truly alert Monarch is always aware that it is his or her duty to prepare the kingdom so that it can carry on successfully after he or she is dead. If this duty – and again it is a loving duty – is carried out successfully the leader will hand over more and more power to others in the actual execution of tasks, and will become a respected repository of wisdom. Such a Monarch transforms into the sixth stage, the **Magician**. Just like the Magician in the Tarot pack, this figure respects the customs and rites of what is holy, will uphold laws and agreements, and will do so in the same way a priest does. A priest of any denomination, merely by existing, can be a re-minder to all of us as to how we should behave and what the highest expectations are for everyone. The Magician doesn't need to say much; the magic gets worked by the actions of the people and their belief in what is good, which really is, of course, another form of love.

And so we see how love grows. We are invited on a journey during which we can move from Innocent, to Orphan, to Pilgrim, to Warrior-Lover, to Monarch, and finally to Magician. Each stage represents a fundamental re-adjustment of the self to the outside world, and no stage can be skipped. At every stage we have to reappraise what love might be. Indeed, whenever we start something new, like a job or a relationship, we're likely to begin as Innocents and work our way up. Sometimes we can get through the first stages quickly because we know ourselves and are alert to what we are doing, but sometimes we can't.

Notes

1. Nick Hornby, *About A Boy* (London: Penguin, 1998). The very successful movie of the same title, starring Hugh Grant, was released in 2002.
2. 'Let them eat cake' is traditionally attributed to Marie Antoinette (1755-93) the consort and queen of Louis XVI of France. However, it was recorded first by Jean Jacques Rousseau in his 12 volume *Confessions*, published in 1770. Since the words appear in volume 6, written in 1767, the unnamed 'great lady' he reports as having spoken them could not have been Marie, as this would have been some three years before she appeared in France.

Chapter Four

The Innocent

❧

What Can the Innocent Teach us?

One could say that the first thing we learn is love. That would be putting it in a misleading fashion, however, since what the newborn baby expresses is probably instinctual – the need to be fed. Closely following that is the need to be held, warmed, and yes, loved. What we observe with mothers and children is such a powerful, primary bond that it's difficult to give it adequate words. Mothers, almost without exception, love their babies with a ferocity that sometimes surprises them. Babies are genetically programmed to love their mothers – it helps their survival rate – and yet what grows from this is surely a wonder to all.

The child learns to cooperate, to feed successfully and just as importantly, discovers how to *be* fed. The gentle to-and-fro rhythm of being rocked and fed, lulled and soothed, is vital if the child is to flourish. Children who are not held and who do not learn how to feed successfully seldom thrive. The baby at the breast learns many lessons at this time, and the results of these primary lessons will help shape major aspects of the psyche for the rest of that child's life. The child learns how to be bonded with – how to love – and that love has a reciprocal component to it. In learning to express needs and in expecting to have them met, the child also learns to honor her inner needs and be optimistic about the outer world's willingness to respond to her. She learns that she is *worthy*, and so she loves herself. The child learns about pleasure, too: all that warm milk makes her feel satisfied and drowsy and the child experiences safety.

All this has been observed, and can be seen in any maternity ward or anywhere that mothers and their young children gather. The absence of this loving acceptance can have surprising results, which is why I consider that this stage is full of important lessons that have to be assimilated before the individual can progress. Children don't learn these important aspects of life haphazardly. They learn through positive exposure to this love. When it doesn't happen, for whatever reason, the upset in the child's emotional growth can be truly damaging. When

I was a young graduate I worked with emotionally disturbed teenagers and I noticed how many of them could not form attachments, did not love themselves, had difficulty trusting, and became anxious around the issue of food. Would there be enough? Would it be safe to eat? Who had prepared it? Their anxieties around such primary issues would often come out as aggressive behaviors.

The most difficult of these young adults were those who had been abandoned at a very early age, whose mothers had never bonded with them, or who had been emotionally deprived because of inadequate parenting, poverty, or a mixture of both. The damage in those very early days had not been fully healed by later successful loving relationships, and so they came to the facility in which I worked as destructive, violent, and self-destructive teenagers who were sometimes entirely unable to accept any responsibility for their own actions. In fact some even had a distorted idea of what cause and effect was. The young man who hot-wired my car and drove it into a tree refused to admit he'd been at the wheel (even though I'd dragged him out from behind it) and then, later, proceeded to blame me for having bad brakes on my car. It was a bizarre experience for me to observe – and I cannot help but think that the primary experience of love and trust that he had never had might have contributed a certain amount to his odd way of viewing the outer world, where there was no connection between events.

Some of the psychological damage can go even deeper. Children who have been abused are more likely to develop multiple personality disorders, sometimes called Dissociative Identity Disorders. Simply stated, if a person experiences a traumatic event (and traumatic events are always the opposite of loving events) there is a shocked reaction within the child that says, in effect, 'This could not have happened to me. It must have happened to someone else.' And so the psyche will create a sub-personality to hold the experience in such a way that it does not overflow into and overwhelm the self-image that already exists. The frightening experience remains sealed off in a separate memory area, and so cannot be easily brought out for consideration – and without that the damage cannot be healed. In a more healthy situation, events that are not pleasant and not loving can be accessed in order to be understood and brought to resolution, often with the loving help of trusted others.

Obviously it's not always possible to point to one aspect of a child's life and pin down a single event that caused the pain, yet we know that early deprivation causes considerable confusion in the growing child's awareness, and that this early deprivation always has an emotional component to it. The experience of reliable love, however, can protect children from the worst effects of trauma. Children can deal with starvation, fear, and dreadful physical deprivation, and still recover quickly. What they can't deal with is the deprivation of reliable and steady love.

As the well-loved child grows he or she lives in a relatively benign world. Ideally the child experiences being loved and provided for, and grows a sense of self-worth as a result. Every meal is a reinforcement of the message: "You matter. We feed you. And you have to fit in and eat pretty much what we eat when we eat it." This caring is reflected in every other activity – from the child being dressed, to being bathed, to being put to bed at an appropriate time, and it builds the child's confidence that the world of parents will care for her. One could call this a sense the child has of entitlement, or one could call it a decision to join a family contract. Either way the love bond the child felt as a helpless infant is not loosened so much as subtly altered. There are expectations and demands that come along with this. With any luck at all, the child accepts the rhythms of life, love, and cooperation.

Of course children are naughty and disobedient, and committing their minor offenses they are, as we say, "testing the limits." They don't do this just to be annoying. What they are really testing is how far love and acceptance go before love turns into something else – loving admonition. Children can be exhausting as they push the boundaries in this way. And yet their fascination with what they can get away with becomes much more understandable when we see it as them trying to find out at what point love turns into its seeming opposite, anger. Since love is the biggest thing in their lives, discovering that it can be turned into something else, something unpleasant, is analogous to us asking how loveable we are. Perhaps that's why we keep returning to it. An adult will play with a lighted candle, prodding it perhaps. 'I do this, it still burns. I do that, it still burns. I do this … oops! I'm now sitting in the dark.' Humans routinely test limits, whether they are athletic limits or speed limits on the freeway. In each case we think, "I'm special, I can get away with this." In each case that sense of being special depends upon the sense of being loved *for our own sakes* that we learned at the breast and in childhood. Think about that next time you're speeding. Probably that's one reason we all seem to resent the traffic cop who tickets us. How could he do this to me? Doesn't he know how late I am already? Yet why should we resent him for doing something that keeps us all safer? We should thank him. It's our sense of "specialness" that prevents us from seeing that situation logically. With six billion people on the planet not one of us is any more "special" than anyone else, and no one is above the law. Yet we still believe we are. Perhaps the experience of being loved sends a powerful message of being special, and it's one that lasts a lifetime.

Lovers do this when they ask each other things like "Will you still love me when I'm old and gray?" It seems childish, and in a sense it is because I have seen children ask similar questions of their parents. I remember distinctly one of my friends at school asking his parents, nervously, about his application to a high level private school: "Even if I don't pass the entrance exam, will you still love me?" The real question is not about the school, but about the need to feel total acceptance by the parent.

The child's ability to feel whole-hearted love, to be fine with being exactly whoever he or she is, becomes a huge advantage when he or she falls in love and forms a life partnership. That ability to trust is vital in any mature relationship. No marriage can work very well or for very long without trust. But what do we mean by trust? Perhaps an example will help. In the movie *Saving Private Ryan*, there is a scene in which a French family is marooned on the upper floor of their house when half of it collapses from a bomb attack. The U.S. soldiers arrive and the French father picks up his daughter, aged about 7, and lifts her down to the soldiers. Just as this happens a shot rings out, the soldiers carry the girl to cover, and the family cowers back in the destroyed room. A firefight ensues and at the end of it the soldiers, fewer in number now, help the civilians down to the ground. The young girl begins screaming at her father, thumping him, yelling that he should not have abandoned her. It's a riveting scene, based on an actual event. It speaks volumes, because what we can see in that brief episode is a child who was frightened but had total trust and love and faith in her father. When he handed her over to strangers she knew the terror of abandonment, the fear of death that she had felt protected from to some extent in his presence. She hits him because he has *betrayed* (as she thinks) all her expectations of him. His love makes him want to save his daughter. Her love makes her attack him asking in effect, "How could you treat my love and faith like that? What kind of a father are you?" The emotion in each case is love and we witness its enormous power. Since the movie as a whole is concerned with issues of trust, loyalty, fraternal love, and what happens to them in the presence of extreme danger it is not whimsical to take this incident and see how it sheds light on these important topics.

Mothers I have spoken with have frequently been astonished at the loving need their babies express as well as at their own maternal stirrings. One woman described her feeling as "ferocious." A less dramatic statement came from a woman who said that the mother-child bond was like "God-love." It's unconditional and unbreakable, even though as the child grows this love becomes transmuted into mere ordinary human love, she explained. Yet the experience of that first love reminded her of what God must have felt when the Creation took place, she said. The creator was the creation, and the creation was part of the creator. There was no separation.

If the stage of the Innocent is to be honored fully then it must be seen not as some Disney moment of saccharine soft focus, with violins in the background. It must be seen in all its primal simplicity and force. The child knows how to love

– and not just because mother is good, or pretty, or can play the piano. The child loves the core of who mother is before the word is even known. If the Hindu greeting "Namasté" – the divine in me greets the divine that is in you – means anything then it probably indicates what goes on, every day, between a mother and her baby.

The arrival of the baby brings the qualities of love, trust, attachment, total faith in the other person, and the unquestioning acceptance of the other into existence in a way that perhaps had not been experienced since the mother was herself a baby. And while these qualities are not a viable strategy for living and getting ahead in our material world today, we may want to ask whether the baby is wrong or the way the world has turned out is wrong. Why shouldn't the baby's innocence win over? The fault is in ourselves.

So let's explore this for a moment. Why is it that this extraordinary love cannot survive?

Both *A Course in Miracles* and the words of Eckhart Tolle suggest that we are in a world in which the ego currently has full sway, and this is what causes us to divert our attention from loving our neighbor because he or she is as we are. We focus instead on how different we are. *A Course in Miracles* tells us that this is the delusion we suffer and it causes separation from our true loving nature. Psychology suggests exactly the same thing, although the orthodox view is that the child's idealizing love comes into sharp conflict with an imperfect world, and so the love has to be muted. This is acceptable and this is normal. If the legends of the exile from the Garden of Eden have psychological truth in them, then it could be said that the fall of Adam and Eve into a world of labor and pain is what we experience when we are divided from this God-love. Every child is flung out of Eden when the demands of the world intrude on the mother-child closeness.

Writer and preacher Frederick Buechner puts this idea of separation in an interesting way. He suggests that even wording such as "God exists" is a contradiction, since to say that God exists is to say that God can stand outside of himself (ex-sistere). If we can imagine a God who exists, we can also imagine a God who does not exist, or who never existed. We could imagine a God with a white flowing beard, sitting above the clouds, who has many attributes including omnipotence, four wheel drive, air conditioning, and cup holders, but not, alas, existence. Yet if God is like a mother giving birth to her children then God is always in those creations just as the mother's flesh and DNA are in her children and will be in her grandchildren, and so on. If God is everything, then everything is God. We only think we have separate existence, and that is where our ego leads us astray. We are all linked, according to such thinking, and when we love our brother we are loving ourselves, since our brother is ourself. Beuchner puts it this way: "God makes the world in love. For one reason or another the world chooses to reject God".

So we could say that God, the ultimate creative force, or whatever one wants to call it, has brought everything into being and, of course, God loves it all – even if we don't always love each other, love the planet, or love the divine mystery that brought us here. This is just like any mother's experience. The child grows, moves away and lives an independent life; yet the mother will always remember those early days when each was everything to the other.

The lessons that the very young child learns are therefore all about love in its most pure and powerful form. It gives us an extra jolt when one considers Jesus' advice that we should be as little children as we go through the world. It's not worldly advice. It won't make you CEO of a Fortune 500 company. It's spiritual advice. We can render unto Caesar what is Caesar's, or we can render unto God what is God's, but at some point we'll have to decide which one we want to put first. If we put pure love first, Jesus said, then we really don't have to worry about worldly things.

The idea is a compelling one. Even a casual glance at nature will reveal to us that animals routinely love their young, although this is not true of all animals. Egg-laying reptiles and fish on the whole have little to do with rearing their offspring, and even some birds are fairly detached from the results of their mating. Only mammals seem to raise young that are dependent on them for a long time, and may in fact become part of the tribe or family for the entire life of the parents. This familial link is something that is most highly developed in primates. Whether we like it or not, whether we believe in God or not, one of the main concerns for humans has to be how to get along with others of our own kind, and so all lessons of life can be boiled down to questions of love. Even in our highly technological society where we can remain in air-conditioned cocoons for much of our time, we still have to interact with others, we still have to have jobs, pay bills, buy food, and agree to abide by all sorts of rather complicated rules that make sure we stay alive and function. Anyone who has ever filled in a tax return knows that. Again and again we are more or less forced to find out how to get along with others. We keep getting steered back to love in some form or another. How well we negotiate this may have a great deal to do with our inherent human tendencies – are we extroverting or introverting; do we have courage or are we afraid of others? Yet it also has a huge amount to do with those lessons we learned at our mother's breast.

The lessons the Innocent can give are available to us all, whenever we choose. We can see aspects of the Innocent in the complete confidence and trust shared between happily married couples. They simply trust each other. Of course, this may come from ignorance or laziness or stupidity – or it may come from real faith in the other. Such faith cannot grow unless each person concerned has faith in himself or herself as being lovable and worthy of respect and expects the same treatment. Notice, it's not a case of the partners having a proportionate trust in each other. It's not a situation where 85% trust is fine. Trust is 100% or not at all. That is the purity of the Innocent's standard.

Yet there is another aspect that needs to be noted. The Innocent will always be the one to forgive easily, sometimes a little too easily – at least as long as she remains an Innocent. The parent will keep taking back the child, the wife will keep taking back the spouse, the child will always wish to forgive the parent's mistreatment, but only up to a point. When that point is reached the individual becomes an Orphan.

Perhaps you could take a moment and observe a mother and infant, or a day-care center, and when you do try to see what goes on in front of you as an exercise in love, however imperfectly it may be expressed. Mothers and fathers may fuss and complain and scold, but they are present, attending, devoted, loving. Babies may scream in distress but once mother appears that anxiety is forgotten in the reassurance of love. It's the most basic form of forgiveness. These lessons are waiting for us everywhere.

The Challenges for the Innocent

Even though the Innocent is the basis of so many important lessons that will be built upon later in life, the particular trap that this archetype can fall into is of refusing to see that there are other lessons. This is the person who will not ask difficult questions and whose response to difficulties is to work harder, offer more support, and undergo more sacrifice. While these are wonderful qualities they are wide open to exploitation. We all have a little of this in us when we cover for another person knowing that this person is abusing our generosity, but we still do it. The Innocent can trust, and occasionally will trust too well or not wisely. Sometimes the Innocent seems incapable of seeing that others might have different standards, and many marriages have suffered because one partner has a far more self-serving sense of what the relationship is, and is permitted to get away with behavior that would be unacceptable elsewhere. Fairy tales and myths are filled with examples of maidens who do not question the erratic deeds of the kings who marry them, and sometimes the women have to be removed from the scene until, by penance, the king earns the right to get them back. The Grimm brothers' *The Girl Without Hands* is a vivid example of this. The girl saves her parents from the devil by allowing her hands to be chopped off. Later the devil forges letters from the king who has married her saying that she is to be killed.

The king's mother intervenes, and sends her away instead. Angels look after her and her hands grow back and, after seven years of searching, her husband finds her again. It's a very odd tale until one chooses to look at it as depicting both the strength and the weakness of the Innocent. She is totally self-sacrificing and her patience and trust do, in the end, defeat the devil and the power of lies, allowing her to become whole again. What is interesting is that her son, whom she takes into exile with her, is called Sorrowful. It is almost as if the Innocent can exist in the world, but only at the price of feeling sadness – and in the end the girl does also need a strong and determined king to look after her. After all, faced with the devil's machinations she loses her hands, which is an obvious indication of how helpless she is initially in the face of deception.

In the tale the girl is both innocent and completely forgiving. In fact the Innocent can teach us that forgiveness is always best given right away, unhesitatingly, exactly as she naturally does, but that it needs to be backed up with self-protective actions. By all means forgive the person who offends you or hurts you, and if that person is not able to understand what forgiveness is and is therefore going to do the same hurtful things again, then the appropriate steps have to be taken to contain or educate or avoid that person. The tale is quite definite about another thing, though, and that is that the story.cannot end happily *without* forgiveness. In some ways it is an extremely accurate tale, for all its stylization. Sorrow will come into the world yet forgiveness changes our relationship to it. To have the girl give birth to a child called Sorrowful, fathered by the one who has hurt her, and to have her love that child despite everything – that indicates the power of love to change evil into good.

Too often we think of the Innocent as someone who is unsuspecting and easily fooled. What we have to recall is that the Innocent is unsuspecting and sees the good in something or someone *first*. This can be a wonderful quality, and it is essentially optimistic. As any of us knows, being around an optimist is not only more fun than being around a pessimist, but it also creates more possibilities for positive interactions with others and therefore creates a better future. Innocents may at times be sad when things go badly, yet they are never likely to be depressed for any length of time. The epidemic of depression and depression-related illnesses in the west could well be linked to the loss of the Innocent optimist in our culture.

Points to Ponder about the Innocent

Perhaps the most important thing to remember about the Innocent stage is that very few people remain in this place for very long because they grow up and face the world and need defenses in place to do that. Yet whenever we start anything new we will, at least for a while, begin at Innocent stage. This can be particularly true when we fall in love. We may wish to make the other person the center of our world just as a child, in a different way, makes a parent the center of her life. One of the commonest complaints heard in social groups of twenty-somethings is that one of their number has been out of contact for a while because he or she has found a new love interest. "Missing in action" is one phrase that gets repeated at such times to describe how someone has given herself entirely over to the experience of the new love, to the exclusion of all her old friends. The thrill of falling in love, the heady delight of feeling that this is really it, comes to some extent from the mobilization of the idealistic Innocent within each of us. This is the point at which we may give too much, and forgive too easily, because we assume the other person is as open and thrilled and starry-eyed as we are. This is, alas, where most people get hurt, because others can exploit their archetypal Innocence. The best possible outcome is when two people get to know each other until they feel safe enough to allow their Innocent archetypes to emerge fully, and at such times there is a powerful, trusting, playful energy between them.

Whether we are falling in love, starting a new job, or making our first major purchase, there is a tendency for us to go into the Innocent phase again. The world tells us to be on our guard, yet if we are too much on the defensive the power of the Innocent cannot emerge to fuel us. We need regularly to be in Innocent stage – when we love our close friends and children, when we nurse them and care for them even if they're being difficult. And it is the Innocent within us that prompts us to imagine new worlds, where poverty can be eradicated, where preventable diseases can be defeated, and where we can exist in harmony. All great humanitarian movements have sprung from the highest version of the Innocent archetype.

Since we all begin as Innocents, and the Innocent represents the purest form of love and trust we can have, it is our task to try and maintain free and ready access to this quality throughout in our lives. This quality in us will grow and develop if we let it. When we reach the Warrior-Lover stage we will know how to use it again more fully, as Innocents in our power to give love but not merely as Innocents since at that point we cannot truly be hurt by those who try to mislead us. Some people never have the chance to experience the Innocent stage. These are the abused and neglected. Yet almost all people can be brought back to this space if given unconditional love and acceptance from others who can access their own, strong Innocent.

In the Bedroom

It's always hard to predict human sexual behavior since one stimulus can produce a variety of responses and expressions, some of which may seem contradictory.

What we need to do is to be aware of what someone does and then try to see what the motivation behind that action might be.

The Innocent – for each time we fall in love we are likely to be in this phase – may at first be shy and reserved, but this archetype can be, in some ways, the most playful and open of all lovers, approaching sex in a wholehearted way that rules out nothing at all in terms of experimentation. Unfortunately, as we've seen, the Innocent tends to get handled roughly by the world and so soon learns the art of self-protection – and in the process stops being the Innocent. One could say that it is the task of a lifetime to allow this most loving archetype to have the courage to step forward again. The Innocent can be re-awakened in each of us when we feel safe, when play feels easy, when there is no judgment to be feared. The Innocent lover will be quick to laugh, will be happy clowning around, and will also bring a purity of emotion to the lovemaking that is free of anxiety. The Innocent, above all, will be unafraid (although this does not rule out some initial shyness) since he or she feels loved and accepted.

Contacting the Energy of the Archetype

Since it's necessary for all of us to value the loving wisdom of the Innocent, it's often a good idea to search out a photograph of yourself at a time when you were happy as a child: trusting, loved, joyous. If you have children or young relatives it can even be a good idea to find a picture or two of those children in a similar state of happiness. Put those pictures somewhere you can see them every day to remind yourself of the lightness and the energy of the Innocent and you will find yourself reconnecting with this aspect of yourself. There are other ways of bringing back this time period into your consciousness, also. Some people have a favorite childhood toy preserved on a shelf, to remind them. Whatever it is you use (and I have a couple of photos and a toy on a shelf in my bedroom that work for me) try to recall the wonder of that time, and the love you felt yourself surrounded by. If your childhood was troubled you may have to use those pictures of your relatives in order to think your way into that place. Once you are aware of it you'll look at children in quite a different way. The toyshop in the Mall will never be the same again!

There are other ways to recapture this sense of wonder. Try watching children in a playground – preferably not as a caretaker or parent but just as an observer. See how they play together. Most of the time they're in a delightful world of joy, fully absorbed in their play. Or go to a pet store and watch the tiny puppies and kittens as they scramble about, trusting and harmless. Notice how you feel. The chances are you'll start to coo at the puppies, you'll smile and want to play with them. Their little teeth on your fingers won't cause you real pain, and you'll forgive them right away if they do hurt you. Imagine if we were always that gentle with others. Imagine if we were like that even when driving in traffic!

A different aspect of the Innocent is when we see the total trust with which children behave with their parents. They walk off with Dad, holding his hand, absolutely confident that the world is a good place and Dad knows where he's going. If you see a parent and child walking along in this way, stop and truly take in what you're observing. How long is it since you've trusted anyone that way? The Gospel hymn, *Put your Hand in the Hand of the Man who Stilled the Water* is hardly transcendent music, but it recaptures part of that spirit and part of our longing to be reconnected to it. Mountain climbers, people who literally give their hands to others whose safety depends upon their trust and skill, know this poignantly. That's probably why so many team-building exercises involve ropes, climbing, and building trust. The Innocent has a deep sense of trust that some of us actually will pay money to recreate. It's all around us if we pay attention.

Being prepared to see the joy and energy and trust of children or of small animals is one way we can reactivate the energy of an archetype within us that we may be tempted to discount simply because it seems as if the world we know has no space for such a creature. We need to make that space.

The Innocent in the Tarot

Before we leave this archetype we need to take a close look at the image from the Tarot that seems to reflect this stage since it can provide some valuable insights. The Tarot has for centuries been regarded as a way of presenting in visual terms various aspects of human situations, some of which can be highly complex. What we'll find is that within the major Arcana of the Tarot we'll be able to see representations of all the six archetypes, in the precise order we're considering them here, although rendered in a slightly different form.

The card that seems to evoke the Innocent best is called The Sun, numbered 19 in the Major Arcana. In the Rider Tarot deck the image is of a very young child, fearlessly riding a horse, hands held out, while the sun blazes behind her. What strikes any observer is the combination of images of strength – the huge sun with a human face, the horse – and the images of weakness seen in the child and the sunflower. Perhaps this is a hint as to the openness, the strength, and the simplicity that we see in the Innocent. No other Tarot card has an infant so prominently placed on it, for example. In fact there are very few children in the Tarot at all. Possibly this is an image we can hold in our minds to help us feel what this stage is all about.

This card is sometimes seen as a card that 'more than anything else indicates the hope for a better future' according to Hali Morag. That would appear to be a good description of the Innocent as the first in the series of important stages. But there is more. Other cards that help to explain it also surround this card.

Number 20 in the deck is 'Judgment,' showing an angel announcing Judgment Day, while number 21 is 'The World' which shows a naked female figure holding two wands, dancing in a wreath of flowers. Take a moment to consider these images. The Day of Judgment announces the end of the world and all worldly things, so it seems fitting that these two cards are side by side contrasting each other. The last card – numbered 0 usually, but sometimes 21, whereupon The World becomes 22 – is The Fool. The Fool has always been regarded as a potent card, showing a young man who is oblivious to the usual rational processes we expect. He hangs what appears to be a rich purse carelessly at the end of his staff, he looks upwards at the sky as he walks towards a precipice, and he seems to be ignoring

the dog at his side. As we see in Shakespeare's *King Lear*, the fool or the court jester is the person we can laugh at and ridicule at first sight, but he is also the one who speaks the truth, who does not subscribe to the values of the material world and who seems more in tune with the eternal. Shakespeare refers often to the idea of the 'wise fool' who is not the same as the 'natural', or the mental defective. For Shakespeare the wise fool is a powerful figure, one who is sufficiently alert not to be taken in by others, and who in some instances can prophesy.

If we take these four cards together we can see that The World is the opposite of Judgment, and The Fool is the irresponsible version of The Sun. The grouping of the cards suggests to us that the strength that exists in the Innocent is not accidental. It depends upon a sense of balance between this world and the next, as well as a sense of being rooted in the here and now which the Fool is not able to achieve. As we've seen, a baby may know about love, but a baby is helpless. The child in The Sun card is not helpless. On the contrary, he is riding a horse and has his hands out as if to balance himself. This suggests that the Innocent's strength is never just instinctual, but that it requires balance, since it is the conscious application of the power of trust and love. It is a power that is not overly concerned with this world, or the next, and has remained sane. This is the confidence of the child to take risks of trusting, as the card has a 'Look Ma, no hands!' type bravado to it. As such the Innocent fears no judgments.

Notice that the figures on the Judgment card do not appear to be afraid either; rather they have their arms open wide to greet the new era. They are the virtuous souls, innocent of guilt, going to heaven. If the Judgment card represents the dawn of the heavenly new era, then The World card should also be seen as signaling a different type of new life, since the garland of flowers is in a vaginal shape around a naked young female figure. This card may well be a fertility image with all the promise of new lives ahead.

At the risk of reducing the cards to very basic meanings, we could say that the cards are telling us as we start out in life that we must find who we are between this world (The World) and the next (Judgment), and that our Innocent qualities have to be recognized and used in a strong, focused way as depicted in The Sun, rather than in the scattered way depicted by The Fool. This fits with all we have been considering. The unloved child will tend to be frightened, and where there is fear there can be no real confidence; and without confidence there can be no learning or growth. The Sun card shows the infant learning to ride, and so represents a stage of personal growth and self-trust.

The three cards that surround The Sun are, it seems, cards that help to clarify what we need to understand about the Innocent. Obviously the Tarot has many different possible interpretations, yet there seems here to be a resonance between this archetype and what we see in the cards of the major Arcana, and the echoes they provide can certainly be described as suggestive. These four cards are at the bottom of the deck of the major Arcana, all clustered together, and so they are fitting as a beginning point – which is what the Innocent is. As we will see there will be many more correspondences and echoes as we proceed through the six stages, and the cards in the Tarot deck mirror these, keeping step with them along the way.

Notes

1. *Saving Private Ryan*, directed by Steven Spielberg, starring Tom Hanks and Tom Sizemore, 1998.
2. *A Course in Miracles*, no author given, The Foundation for Inner Peace, (New York: Penguin, 1996).
3. Eckhart Tolle, *The Power of Now: A Guide to Spiritual Enlightenment* (Novato CA: New World Library, 1999). See also his *A New Earth: Awakening Your Life's Purpose* (New York: Plume, Penguin, 2005).
4. Frederick Beuchner, *Now and Then* (HarperSanFrancisco, 1985). p. 20.
5. Jesus, in Matthew 18, 3. "Verily I say unto you, Except ye be converted, and become as little children, ye shall not enter into the kingdom of heaven."
6. *The Girl without Hands* is tale 31 in *The Complete Grimm's Fairy Tales*, trans. Margaret Hunt (New York, Pantheon Books, 1944, revised 1970), pp.160-165. Commentary is provided in this volume by Joseph Campbell.
7. *Put Your Hand in the Hand*. This Gospel hymn was written by Gene MacLellan and popularized by the band *Ocean* with their million selling single in 1971.
8. Hali Morag, *The Complete Guide to Tarot Reading* (Astrolog, 1998), p.48.
9. The figure of the wise fool appears in *King Lear, Twelfth Night, As You Like It*, and in a different version in *Hamlet*, to mention just the most obvious examples.

Chapter Five

Orphan Love

❧

The Orphan is in a different position from the Innocent, and knows it. The love that the Innocent feels naturally has been threatened, perhaps broken completely. This doesn't have to be dramatic; for example often the Orphan may feel she doesn't quite belong to the family unit as she grows up. This is the time when children look at their parents and hope that they are, in fact adopted, because they feel so little connection with the things those parents seem to care about. This is a natural part of growing up as the agreements that worked for the child have to be readjusted at around the age of 11 or so, and sometimes earlier. The result of this can be, occasionally, that the child doubts that she is loved, or loveable, and feels this as conflict. How can she need so much and be so dependent on people who don't seem to know who she is? Why do they give her a cell phone and then get so angry about the bill? Don't they know how important it is for her to contact her friends? So rebellion and the desire to conform are two edges of the same blade.

Teenagers find this situation almost impossible at times and we can learn a great deal by observing their situation. Parents want them to be one thing; school teachers want them to be something slightly different; coaches want them to focus on the game *first;* and their peers want them, need them, to form cliques. These are powerfully persuasive groups, and elicit powerful feelings. Faced with all these demands to be a certain way, the teenager makes choices. She joins a clique, a club, a gang, and clings to that identity as one of the truly important aspects of her life. Perhaps this is genetically coded. Perhaps our ancestors had to stick together as adolescents because even though adolescents tend to take risks, the more there are of them in one place the better the chance that most of them will survive long enough to reproduce.

This "group-think" attachment may not feel much like love, but the adolescents involved often seem ready to be together in risky circumstances, and are sometimes ready to die for each other, as our newspapers report fairly regularly. So it may not actually be love as much as a desperate need to belong. Yet it looks a lot like love.

Adults can feel the same way about their lives; they need the job but hate it; they've fought to make the career they no longer believe in; they've worked at the marriage, yet they don't feel it's quite right, or not a good fit in some way for the whole of who they are.

This is the realm of the Orphan and many of us will spend many years in this stage, trying to fit in as well as we know how. If we can achieve this, we can reach the balanced stage of this archetype where we realize that the world is far from perfect but we must get on and make the best of it that we can. The balanced Orphans of our world are often loving and devoted people, frequently in the helping professions of medicine or social work, and our world depends upon them. Orphans who do not achieve this sense of balance will often feel discontented, sometimes hankering after the next new acquisition that will make them feel complete, and always slightly disappointed as a result since a sense of completeness is not something that can ever be bought. The saddest version of the unbalanced Orphan is the person who belives that someone will come along to love and rescue them and make them happy. Since no one can make us happy (we have to do that for ourselves) this is a figure who is inevitably disappointed.

In order to avoid this sense of discontent the Orphan often finds it necessary to select a group or a situation to belong to. Since the Orphan is looking for a 'home' to be adopted into, those who enter this phase can be fiercely loyal to their workplace, their home, and their social circles.

College roommates, boarding school chums, basic training recruits, those who went to the same primary and secondary school – all of them feel bound by a tie that is seldom matched by other friendships. And this is not to be under-estimated: Orphans know how to make friends. For this is the basic strength of the Orphan's sense of love – it goes deep and is a response to the depth of need that has inspired it. But because it stems from need it is, in the end, often a product of conventional thinking. So for the Orphan the loved one may well have to fulfill certain expectations, which are largely those of the social grouping the Orphan has agreed to be adopted into. Friends are expected to do the same things the same way. And when it comes to public events the pressure is even greater. The prom, the dance, even the wedding must be a certain way, perhaps; the ring has to be of a specific type or size, and the loved one must be acceptable to the particular group that is most valued. That group may or may not include parents and relatives, but its dictates will be powerful.

The TV reality show 'Bridezillas' is a splendid and unpleasant reminder of this, since it shows brides preparing for their weddings and having nervous breakdowns over the things that in their eyes are not just perfect. The napkins are folded wrongly? Meltdown! The flowers have too many lilies in them? Watch the rage erupt! The TV audience is encouraged to see these frantic women as monsters, temporarily insane, and certainly as unlikely candidates for happiness ever after. They are in reality just Orphans who are frightened of being judged by other Orphans and who have internalized a sense of this by constructing the ideal of what 'should' be. The fear of judgment by the peer group is a particular challenge for the Orphan and the high TV ratings seem to suggest that people in general have no trouble empathizing with some aspects of their behavior.

The Orphan tends to choose by assessing the outer qualities first, reaching for inner qualities only with some fear and reluctance. The children at the boarding school I attended in England when I was young – all Orphans figuratively – clung to each other awkwardly because we all felt, to some extent, abandoned. And that was the very fact none of us would admit. So we acted with bravado, we tried to show we were not worried by anything, but in the end the people we knew we had to fit in with were those classmates who accepted us, at least for now.

As a direct result Orphan love can be unquestioning; it can look like blind faith. The young man who joins a gang may not be expressing a need much different than the woman who joins the Marines. Both want to belong. Both want prestige, and both want respect according to someone else's definitions. These are the people who play by their group's rules, who help their world run in a predictable way. Their love – for it is love – is based on the deep-seated need for the safety of a system. To get it they will suppress many of their natural qualities and feelings.

This love is, in some ways, untested. Testing it would lead to questions, and questions would lead to reevaluation.

The Orphan's Challenges:
Resentments

The point of change for the Orphan who wishes to grow is to remain aware that this loving attachment, this self-serving, secure version of altruism, is not the ultimate expression of who she can be. For Orphans tend to cling to the identity they have had to construct. Consequently Orphans have trouble forgiving others, since they hold onto a sense of identity that is so fragile that, when they are hurt, it becomes necessary for them to grasp hold of their wounds tightly and remember them. Without their injuries and losses they may become fearful about who they are, and letting go of hurts is what forgiveness is all about. Forgiveness involves dissolving the sense of personal affront that we all tend to cling on to, and for an Orphan that sense of ego-based pride is very strong. The Orphan will always find it easier to hold on to a grudge than to let it go. Making or discovering an authentic identity is not something Orphans can begin to imagine doing, so they often cherish their woundedness. Healing can be difficult for most of us when we are in Orphan stage.

If you find yourself unable to let go of grudges or old hurts (and which of us doesn't have a few of those?) you may want to think of yourself as having temporarily become an Orphan in this part of your life. The task then becomes to imagine who you could be if you were to let go of these old hurts.

It is very easy for anyone to become stuck in this sense of victim-hood. One young woman I worked with, who had graduated from an Ivy League college, could not let go of the hurts she felt she had suffered at the hands of her relatively benign parents. In order to feel her own sense of identity as a young adult she had found it necessary to reject certain aspects of her parents' religious faith, and she had become an Orphan from their values. For a while her college friendships had sustained her, but as those people gradually moved away to begin their own lives she found herself more and more alone, still living a 'student' life, working in a local college's administrative structure as a secretary. She had begun the work of establishing her own identity – she had rebelled and left the beliefs of her home behind – but then she had got stuck and found it difficult to continue her search for who she might be. She blamed her lack of ability to move forward on her 'messed-up childhood' as she described it. The more she did this the stronger her sense of identity as a victim became. And while she nursed that sense of outrage and sorrow she had the persuasive excuse that of course she couldn't grow because she had been so poorly treated as a child and young adult. Her Orphan identity, instead of being just a stage she could move through, had become a refuge sufficient for her needs.

Normally this would not be a problem. Many Orphans find an identity this way and like-thinking friends to go with it. They live their lives relatively successfully within the box they have chosen and are able to find substantial happiness. In this way Orphans can live productive and fulfilling lives. In the case of this young woman what I saw was the unhappiness of her present experience. She knew there was more to her life, but she was afraid to move away from the carefully-built defenses she had lavished so much time upon. Worse still, from my point of view, was that her considerable intelligence allowed her to find plentiful, persuasive reasons for not changing anything. Moving her apartment was a major trauma for her. Changing her job – a job that she hated – felt impossible; she had become too comfortable complaining about it to be able to change and seek genuine fulfillment.

She had come to me seeking change, but she could not really face what change would mean. My task was to encourage her to feel that whatever choice she made, changing or not changing, she was choosing it, herself. I do not think we were successful in dealing with this. She was so well-defended that it was a point she could not see. Almost every session she was able to produce yet another example of how someone had 'done' something to which she was now forced to respond, and to which she could find no way to respond adequately. The pattern was clear to me, but not, alas, to her. If she had been able to see that she had some responsibility for some of the things in her life, then she would have seen that there were more things in her life she could take control of; but that would have meant she was in charge of her life and she couldn't face that.

And there is nothing whatsoever wrong with this way of being. This young woman had a need to be an Orphan, yet she could see her friends advancing in their lives and she felt that they were judging her. Rather than form her own assessment, she took her cue from them and judged herself as lacking. She wasn't able to move forward, but now she had taken on a sense of guilt about that, so she couldn't reach a place of peace with her Orphan status. Thus she developed into an unhappy Orphan, feeling trapped, blaming others – always blaming others – and turning all the real delights of our marvelous world into ashes.

This example may sound extreme, but in fact it isn't. It's remarkably common. When Thoreau described his fellow citizens of the Commonwealth of Massachusetts as living "lives of quiet desperation" I believe he was describing something similar, and something very prevalent at any point in history. For the fact seems to be that Orphan identity can take us over so that we do not feel the strengths we really have, and therefore we cannot change or grow.

So what does this have to do with love?

The Orphan who remains more attached to outer influences than to a sense of inner authenticity has failed to love herself first. She does love herself, to some extent, but she puts the demands of the group, of orthodoxy, first. And so the failure to move away from Orphan status is truly a shortfall of love and a belief in the vital nature of that love. What we need to take away from this is that Orphans, in failing to love themselves first, fail to achieve real inner courage. This does not mean that they cannot be brave, for they will be vehement in support of the existing status quo and sometimes they will be furious if it seems likely they will be asked to let go of their beloved misery. This is quite different, however, from loving oneself, knowing oneself, and insisting on being oneself. Orphans, therefore, sometimes attach to situations that solve the immediate problem of loving and needing to belong, but at the cost of offering no real possibility for development.

An example that springs to mind is the character of Bree from *Desperate Housewives*. This is a character we all love to hate, yet we've all met exactly this type of person, one who resolutely clings to order, appearances, and control no matter what. No one who knows this series will forget Bree holding up her husband's funeral in order to change his tie before the coffin is shut – replacing the orange and green prep school tie placed there by Rex's mother with a tie she has demanded from one of the congregation. She shows considerable courage in doing this: useless courage, since her husband will be buried in the next few minutes. Appearance matters to her. The action is bizarre, but it feels true in a general sense as a representation of all those people who put appearances before everything else. This is the Orphan's desire to fit in – a desire echoed by other characters in the series. Most of the characters in this long-running show seem to behave as Orphans most of the time, since they are only out for themselves and their limited goals of winning prestige or supremacy over their neighbors. They fight and bicker and their children resort to disturbed behavior, and they seem surprised by this.

Consider a more extreme situation: in a gang the identity of the group is so strong that anyone who tries to leave is seen as disloyal, sometimes fit only to be killed. The Mafia enforces loyalty unto death, and interestingly the Marine Corps motto *Semper Fidelis* means 'always faithful.' It is a mirror of a similar type of attachment: once a Marine always a Marine, is the saying, and the 'adoption' is a source of tremendous pride for these serving men and women.

This attachment to some form of orthodoxy, whether to a socially acceptable group, a religious group, or to a criminal group, has been in our society for a very long time. Obviously we all hope that the more productive adoptions will prevail; yet these are, in their basics, simply different expressions of the same impulse. What we may want to realize is that it is not the only way to live.

Orphans may not always seem to demonstrate the highest expression of love and loyalty, yet they are by no means to be disregarded. These are the people who will fight for their love, their homeland and their beliefs, even if it means destroying the things they love in the process. When someone threatens those things we hold dear we are all likely to become Orphans in our thinking, trying to do our duty to protect the way of life we cherish. We can be in awe of this powerful devotion, and frightened by our reluctance to question what it is we are doing.

As citizens who care about their society, Orphans will very often be excellent organizers of programs for the community and they will be deeply reliable, decent people. They are what keeps society stable and inside each one is the possibility of an emerging figure that is even more vitally engaged in spiritual growth.

So what keeps an Orphan as an Orphan?

To some extent it is mere habit. Everyone else seems to be doing the same thing and to be different leaves one feeling slightly crazy. The biggest item, however, is ego. Ego is constructed when we take in the messages the outside world sends us about who we are: at grade school we learn we're not as tall as Sally, can't paint as well as Billy and that we're a better catcher than Ivan. And so we allow others to tell us who we are, rather than trusting our internal processes as they unfold. The Orphan accepts this diagnosis, where the Pilgrim will question it.

Further Challenges: the Trap of Orphan-thinking

Orphans are all around us, and many of them are decent people, perhaps even our good friends. To some extent we all accept the Orphan stage since we agree to accept the rules of our society and we wish to continue to be part of it. As we describe Orphans here there will be a temptation for me as writer and you as reader to want to see things the way the Orphan sees our world. After all, we've all been Orphans, no matter where we are now, and we know only too well how to rationalize the situation.

If you're reading this book you are probably already a discontented Orphan or a Pilgrim who is searching for other or better answers. The important thing is not to slip back into the seductive world view of the Orphan but to grow beyond it. For Orphan-think is all around us, every day, tempting us back into limited existence.

The most important thing to recall about the Orphan stage is that it is a form of culturally-sanctioned behavior caused by laziness or fear (and they are linked characteristics) that is fueled by the messages sent by the ego. It is the ego that tells us we have to buy the latest accessory so we can be just a shade better than everyone else, and that this will make us happy. It is the ego that insists on being right rather than being loving, open and accepting. It is the ego that wants to demonize minorities or those with other beliefs so that we can feel more enlightened, more right. The ego tells us we are little and insignificant unless we assert ourselves over others. Get that promotion! This company is for winners not losers! Yet, truly, if anyone gains success at the expense of someone else *losing* something, there are no winners. If we focus only on what we can achieve within an accepted sphere of action we are, in effect, limiting ourselves, making ourselves little rather than great. I have witnessed bitter fights for the chairperson's job in tiny organizations, vicious campaign tactics when running for the presidency of the local golf club, and I've had to ask if such a small victory really calls for such a ruthless effort. This is the ego belief in our own littleness and it keeps us playing inside the box, where we solace ourselves with feeling big yet fearing that we are small. It is a myopic stance, and unhealthy.

For we are not small. We are all growing, if we allow ourselves to do so, and it is only the fear that we are unlovable that keeps us feeling small. If we really *felt* lovable, we wouldn't spend so much time trying to make ourselves look better so others would admire and perhaps love us. If we could love ourselves, fully, we wouldn't find the Orphan stage so attractive and its rewards would have few temptations for us.

In order to grow we have to leave that familiar, friendly small box, whether it is home, our home town, our small expectations for ourselves, or a limiting relationship that asks us to mute who we are. This is the way to reject the spiritual restrictions of the Orphan. Orphans are like caged birds that are masters of their realm, sing beautifully, and bring joy; yet they cannot leave the cage, cannot identify food in the wild and cannot survive on their own. Notice how those poor *Desperate Housewives* characters never seem to leave Wisteria Lane for long. If they do they seem to return only in order to try to sleep with someone else's spouse. They keep buying into the same game. It's almost as if they can't bear to be away, because they then would be unable to score points off each other.

The Orphan is the source of all limiting beliefs, all small ambitions. This is the girl or boy next door who will marry and be a fine spouse and parent but with whom the Pilgrim will feel imprisoned. There are many examples of this sort of limited thinking. Who hasn't known a person who has a relationship to one or other parent that seems to get in the way of his or her own emotional life? The woman who has her mother as her best friend and who is constantly involved in the parent's home life may have moved out of the house but she has never actually left home. Or think of the man whose mother looks after him so well that no other woman can get close, and so he never marries. Such a person is usually quite contented, and has left no room for anyone else, anyone new, to come into his life, and so not much growth is possible.

The Orphan is also the figure who is most likely to manifest physical greed or possessiveness, since when one's ego-identity is caught up in what one owns then anyone who rivals that is seen as a threat to one's existence, and therefore is a potential rival and enemy. Jealousy, controlling behavior, the desire to limit the loved one, to disapprove of the loved one's personal progress – all these are extreme but coherent expressions of the Orphan's fear, and it is fear that limits love. In relationships where one partner is controlling or even abusive the impulse comes, very often, from the dominant person's feeling that the other cannot be allowed any freedom of expression for fear he or she will exploit it and leave. In fearing the loss of the loved one, love itself is destroyed.

Most of the world is made up of Orphans who are convinced that there is no other way to be. This can be extremely dangerous since the noblest, most loving impulses can so easily be channeled into restrictive and oppressive orthodoxy. Both Islamic and Christian fundamentalists alike really believe that they are doing the right thing and that their actions are in tune with God's will, as others have relayed it to them. Indeed, parts of the Bible and Koran make definitive statements, but even a casual reading of the whole of either will reveal contradictions that demand the reader think a little before deciding.

The Orphan stage is therefore simultaneously the most dangerous stage and the most hopeful stage, since recoiling from questions into orthodoxy is at least an acknowledgement that questions exist, even if it is a refusal to engage with them.

As Orphans we tend to internalize the messages the group we belong to tells us about ourselves. We adopt these messages, which is a great loss, especially as some of the messages aren't even true. I cannot begin to count the number of students who have confessed to me that they were told by teachers, parents, and psychiatrists that they'd never graduate high school. Often they've told me this as they're graduating from college. Yet for years they had believed this unsuccessful version of themselves to be the only true representation of who they were; so they struggled with the very notion of success, suffering with low self-confidence and refusing to accept their real achievements. In some cases they actually felt more comfortable failing than succeeding, so strong was the message they'd internalized.

When we believe others' views of who we are, we tend to stop being our authentic selves. Fear of peer ridicule runs deep. Ask any man who "doesn't dance" at a party and you'll see what I mean; yet any three-year-old will dance, spontaneously, not caring who sees.

The ego is not all bad, of course. We construct it as we find out who we truly are, since it allows us to develop a sense of what we are good at, what we enjoy, and what we'd like to do. Unfortunately this newly-constructed ego can be subverted very quickly, so that we operate out of a fear of judgment and we stop believing we are acceptable or loveable just as we are. We begin to believe we can become acceptable only if we do whatever it is the culture demands we do. And so Orphans adopt some very odd behaviors because in the place they live this conduct is the norm.

Points to Ponder

Being an Orphan is a rational response to a difficult world. It makes perfect sense. But it can become a self-imposed prison.

Orphans will be excellent at identifying those who are adrift and welcoming them. The "Lost Boys of the Sudan," thousands of whom were forced to flee because of the civil war, cared for each other during their terrible ordeal; and "The Fishing Boys of Ghana", who were to all intents and purposes slaves, saw their fellow sufferers as brothers whether or not they were actually related. Similarly, Orphans throughout the rest of society club together to make meaningful connections with each other, and they can be generous and loving in a way that is inspiring. Yet they remain bound by a sense of being who they are because the ego tells them not to express themselves fully, but to fit in. Perhaps this is the source of those mid-life crises we hear about – the Orphan finally breaks out, though sometimes into a new, even more conventional phase. The stolid banker who buys a Harley and gets a tattoo is such a cliché; and there are plenty of clichés to be seen around us. One role has been rejected, only for the individual to dive into another role that is just as restricting.

Society depends upon Orphans, people who play by the rules and who care what others think. Gauguin may have run off to Tahiti to paint immortal pictures, but what about the wife and children he left behind? Often the Orphans' condemnations of those who have left their ranks have some real value. And think about those famous words of Nobel Prize winner William Faulkner: "If a writer has to rob his mother, he will not hesitate. The 'Ode on a Grecian Urn' is worth any number of old ladies."

Strong words, yet which of us would feel we could rob our mothers without a pang of guilt? What law court would uphold the artist's claims against a conviction for robbery? Yet I can't help agreeing that Faulkner has a good point.

As Orphans, for we will all be in this stage, we get repeated invitations to explore life further, and the tendency is to turn them all down as too disruptive to our existing values. For example, in our twenties and thirties we may find that having children catapults us into a new sense of what love can be. The wonder of parenthood and the consequent shift in the relationship with our partner forces us to notice that we no longer have time for all the consoling aspects of the life we used to know. Our own parents may become involved with their grandchildren, and they may offer welcome advice or interference, or even a mixture of both. Certainly our lives may not feel as if they are our own any longer, and our definition of what love is deepens. In response we can feel ourselves part of a larger society, which we are, and which we know ourselves to be a part of as we take our children to school and meet the parents of their little friends, and so on. This offers many opportunities for explorations of who we could be. Personal growth is freely available, and yet there is also the temptation to fit in and do as others say we should do. And that's how we become Orphans again.

Some people do not stay in this conventional space. They ask what this experience might be about, even before they become involved with family life, and consider what love might mean for them. Then they begin exploring and become Pilgrims.

In the Bedroom

As with any of these archetypes, behaviors can be contradictory even though prompted by the same stimulus and, with this in mind, we can make a number of general statements about the Orphan.

The Orphan tends to value sex and love-making for its reassuring qualities. Sex can be seen as comfort, as security, and it needs to be reasonably regular, even predictable. This is not to say that the Orphan lover doesn't want to try out new ways to make love and to feel physical pleasure, but the emphasis is on the physical attraction and fulfillment rather than the spiritual or emotional satisfaction. An Orphan wants to feel wanted, to receive pleasure, and wants to know that as far as the partner is concerned she or he is good at what they do. Sex and sexuality are seen in roughly the same way as any major purchase – it has to be quality; it has to be easily recognized as quality according to widely held standards; and it has to provide a sense of security. Often a physically attractive partner is an important aspect, and these are the lovers who will particularly value the exotic locale or the plush hotel suite their partner has arranged for them, since it reassures them that they are cared for. The accoutrements of the relationship are the outward demonstrations that the Orphan needs; the huge diamond ring is worn proudly, even flaunted, as an external sign of being valued. And the list goes on.

Please remember, as you read this, that we all of us have this desire for reassurance that I'm describing as the realm of the Orphan. We all want these very same things – the attractive loving partner, the luxurious bedroom, and so on. What makes the difference is that the Orphan will tend to see these qualities as some of the most important aspects of the relationship. An example might help, here. In Milan Kundera's novel *The Book of Laughter and Forgetting* the main character becomes obsessed by the memory that he once loved a woman who was not beautiful. He can't reconcile this fact with his more usual standards for choosing lovers. He tries to erase the memory but he can't. As he ponders this he finds himself more and more discontented with his normal, conformist, life until he discovers his attitude has made him an object of suspicion for the secret police. His rejection of accepted standards has made him politically dangerous, as he leaves the Orphan world behind and becomes a Pilgrim; it's a tidy metaphor.

In contrast to this there was an amusingly embarrassing example of the way Orphans can think on Oprah's show some years ago. A woman, who didn't realize she was on live TV, claimed that she had refused her boyfriend's proposal of marriage because, as she said, 'You don't make enough money and you're not good enough in bed.' Millions of viewers heard that nugget. So – would she have married him if he had been rich and virile? Is that all she needed? Where was love in this?

For some Orphans this desire for worldly goods and security can even exist when there is very little sex happening. There are many very contented marriages that work even though there is not much sex, but the couple is secure with each other's lack of physical need. They have agreed, it would seem, that the relationship is 'good enough' and that is what they want. This can, of course, be a potential point of conflict since one partner may begin to feel that he or she is not getting enough sex, and this then leads to finding other routes to satisfaction, which is where the discontented Orphan begins to emerge. I suspect this is what lies behind the huge amount of pornography available on the net. Pornography is for some people a relatively risk-free way of getting some physical excitement without upsetting the domestic applecart, and the physical need is dealt with although the spiritual need is not.

The phenomenon of the movie star is likewise interesting when seen in this light, since in the 1980s and 90s the stars of the James Bond movies, for example, were men who acted out the male fantasy of someone who 'got' a large amount of sex. Orphans would very likely be attracted to such a figure since Orphans are often obsessed with how much of anything they have, or can get. In the internet age it seems as if all the glamourous stars are now female – we have only to think of Lindsay Lohan, Paris Hilton, Britney Spears, and Jessica Simpson as figures whose appeal seems chiefly to be that they are young, beautiful, and indiscreet about their personal lives. To this we could add the core of four or five glamourous women who in each case make up the main characters of *Desperate Housewives* and *Sex and the City*. Could this be because men (who are also the most energetic users of pornography) are now following an actress or celebrity to whom they attach on-going fantasies? These fantasies are never likely to conflict with the everyday world. Again, sex is made spiritually irrelevant, although excitement and stimulation exist aplenty, and that is a tendency that is always present for Orphans. Orphans go for the safe option every time.

This attachment to fantasy is present in another version of the Orphan: the obsessive who becomes a stalker. Stalking a famous person whom one has barely met must require a huge amount of mental effort as well as time. The stalker has to *believe* that he or she really has a special relationship with the victim, even though no such relationship exists. A different version of this is the person who cannot accept that a relationship has ended, and it sometimes takes a restraining order to get such a person to wake up. Clearly these actions are based in a refusal to admit that a situation has changed, or that the other person is an independent individual. It's a mental disease that needs treatment, and it's based on the

Orphan's sense of fear and anger that the world is not as he or she would wish. It's a condition that can easily slip into psychosis.

It may seem as if I have been rather hard on Orphans in this section, and that has not been my intent. Perfectly good relationships prosper everywhere in which sex is seen as comfortable and familiar rather than vital and exhilarating, or deeply moving. Similarly, there is anecdotal evidence that there are some sexual relationships which are blisteringly hot, and yet they seem to be able to be that way *because* there is an acknowledged lack of real caring on each side. Clients in my counseling practice have reported to me that they or their peers will sometime seek reliable 'sex-buddies' as a stop-gap when they are hoping to find more meaningful relationships that seem to be harder to achieve. Evidence in each case is largely anecdotal and sometimes accompanied by boasting. We've probably all heard some version of the claim that 'the best sex of my life' was with someone the individual hardly even knew, or met briefly on vacation, or some variant of that. As such the event never becomes fully real. It remains in the realm of fantasy. One night of hot sex with a stranger is not the highest expression of loving attachment. Orphans want the fantasy, but they also need the security of the familiar. They may drool over the Hollywood stars at the movies, but they'll go home contentedly with their spouses.

It's not so much what happens between the people most intimately concerned, but the attitude they bring to what they do that makes all the difference. The Orphan values the physical pleasures, but does not want to have to look too deeply into what it all means.

Choosing the Energy of the Archetype

The Orphan's energy may seem to be somewhat confused, but it still needs to be *felt* in order to be understood. In fact, the Orphan has two aspects and therefore two energies; one is balanced and the other is unbalanced and negative. It's easy – all too easy – to connect with the discontented and negative Orphan in each of us. All we have to do is recall a time we felt angry and misunderstood by those around us, especially at work. We all know how powerful that feeling is! It can have us muttering and growling, and it can take over our lives. I don't think any of us need to spend any more time in that space. We have to remind ourselves to choose only the productive aspect of this and of every archetype. Instead of going towards the pain of feeling excluded and hurt it is a far better idea to recall a time when you were a positive, balanced Orphan. The best way to do that is for you to think of an occasion when you felt like an outsider who was welcomed and loved by someone in an unexpected way. Spend a few minutes thinking about this. Jot down a couple of examples on a piece of paper. How reluctant were you to meet the strangers? What did it feel like? Once you begin to think about it you'll remember many more examples than you expect. I find it immensely consoling to recall the times when relative strangers have welcomed me and been kind. When I was a young man traveling in Europe with almost no money, I was constantly astonished and moved by the open-hearted acceptance I received from those whose language I could barely speak, people who shared their bread and cheese in rattling railcars, or who just seemed interested in bringing me into their family circle, if only for a while. I can recall kindly people who showed me the ropes at new jobs, and who shared a few laughs in the process. This is the power of the balanced Orphan's sense of love. It's about acceptance despite differences. Orphans know how to dissolve those artificial boundaries. Think of the kindly person who gave you directions, who helped you with groceries when the bag split open, or who told you where the best parking spot was to be found. Once you're alert to this the strength and real power of Orphan love is everywhere. You can't miss it. Kindness exists plentifully everywhere if we care to notice it. It's always an energy that we have to choose for ourselves, because the negative and gloomy energy is there waiting to trap us if we don't take care.

It's simple to contact this energy. Do something considerate for a neighbor such as picking up a trash barrel when it gets knocked over. Let someone in a rush go first when you're standing in line at the grocery store. Share something with a colleague. One of the administrative assistants at the college I work for keeps popsicles in the icebox of the communal fridge especially for the maintenance crew. They love that little attention, and they always come right round to fix things when asked.

The Orphans Around Us

Think for a moment of situation comedies and TV dramas. Now think of the people who watch them. One of the main points about so many of these TV series is that the characters do not develop. We know that Joey in *Friends* will always be stupid, and we know that Gabrielle in *Desperate Housewives* will always be self-serving and manipulative. The nature of the series demands it. If the balance is to be maintained then no one can change fundamentally. While this is a technique that is guaranteed to bring us viewing pleasure according to a tried and true formula, we also need to be sensitive to our own desires to be surprised, but only within limits. We want to be able to look at the screen and know, within seconds, just who someone is and how we're supposed to react. Kramer from *Seinfeld* appears on screen and we know what to think, and when Elaine walks in we know she'll always be self-absorbed. This easy recognition is partly a relief for us, because in life we don't always know who people are quite so quickly. We make the easy identification and feel good about ourselves. We feel superior. This is when we slip into Orphan thinking.

So ask yourself, who are the people you know who are addicted to these soaps? The ones who pick up the phone after each episode to discuss the plot with their friends, perhaps? Orphans love to judge Orphans by their own, shared standards. In doing so they confirm what those standards are, and reinforce them. Orphans also love quick answers and so tend to choose situations where there are easily-defined responses, and TV is only too willing to oblige. Complexity and depth leave the Orphan thinker distressed; unfortunately these two elements are always waiting for us.

The Orphan in the Tarot

If we look at the Tarot for hints as to how we can visualize this stage, I'd point to two cards that seem to reflect different aspects. These are The Tower, number 16 in the major Arcana, and The Moon, which is number 18. Take a moment to look at the images now. The Tower is a frightful picture of a castle tower that has been struck by lightning, is on fire, and the inhabitants (who in some versions look like a man and a woman, often with crowns that might suggest a king and a queen) are falling to their deaths. The tower of safety built by this royal pair is no match for the anger of the elements, or the power of God. The top of the tower is in fact a crown, which has been blasted off, suggesting that hiding behind the illusions of class superiority and

possessions will not save anyone. As an image of being cast out of an idyllic place it echoes the Orphan's worst fears, as well as commenting on what Orphans tend to do to avoid their fears – they manufacture a strong home in order to feel secure.

Card 18, called The Moon, is even more poignant as it shows a dog and a wolf stranded between two towers howling at a female figure whose face appears in the moon. Dogs, like Orphans, are miserable without attachment, and wolves are traditionally associated with exile and loneliness, while the two distant towers seem to indicate that even though homes exist these animals don't have them. They are exiles, longing for the eternal mother, who in this image (like the moon itself) waxes and wanes, and seems to be unreliable. Worse still is that dogs, despite being close cousins of wolves, were traditionally used to guard against them. These exiles are in fact sworn enemies. If anything could symbolize the Orphan's way of despising those who are just a little different, or who belong to a different pack, this would be it. Down the middle of the card is a long winding road leading towards the hills. The only creature that seems to be interested in this road is the figure of the lobster (usually referred to as a crab for some reason) that is struggling out of the pool. Obviously the lobster is not going to get very far on that dry rocky path, and so the image signals to us a sense of hopelessness, that it cannot progress spiritually even if it wants to. Lobsters and crabs live inside their armor, and so suggest the defenses the Orphan tends to want to construct for herself. Both of these cards are images of the yearning to belong, to be safe, which is threatened by the realities of changing circumstances.

When those circumstances change, when we are catapulted out of our comfortable lives, we are offered the chance to grow. We are offered the opportunity to move beyond the Orphan world, and to set out like the lobster/crab on a journey that demands we become something different. And if we refuse to do so we stay as lost dogs, howling at the moon, complaining about our fate.

Between these two cards is number 17, The Star.

The first thing we notice is a female figure pouring water from two pitchers. One hand pours water into a pool, the other pours the water onto the shore; one foot is on land, the other in the water. Perhaps the hint is that one can merge one's personality with others in the same way as a jug of water becomes mixed in with the water in the pool, and one can also choose to pour oneself elsewhere, claiming one's own space, although ultimately the waters will flow back to the pool. If this is the balance of the healthy and well-adjusted Orphan then it is an image that steers us to think of how the Orphan wants to blend in and also wants to be different, although not so very different. It seems to be a card that describes the balanced Orphan with astonishing exactitude. Behind the naked figure are seven small stars and one large star – the constellation of the plow and the Pole star are suggested. The Orphan has guidance towards the next stage, but only if she wishes to turn and see it. Behind her the bird in the tree has its wings ready for flight – but is not yet flying. So we could see this card as the Orphan on the cusp of change, ready to move ahead. The name sometimes given to this card is 'the well of the waters of life.' The name reminds us that the balanced Orphans of the world keep society running smoothly, as they care about their social group. But even better than this is the impression that the balanced Orphan will be the figure who will, when ready, venture forward to become a Pilgrim.

Again, the Tarot seems to have given us a series of cards that describe this specific archetypal stage with some elegance, both the good and the negative aspects.

Examples from real life: Princess Diana

Princess Diana's life story can show us some fascinating aspects of the Orphan's world, if we choose to see them. Diana was the typical Innocent when she married Prince Charles; he was 31 and she was 19. She was definitely in love with him – she'd met him as a very young girl and decided he was the one for her – and certainly she was sexually innocent. As a kindergarten teacher she spent her time, happily, with other Innocents. She cannot have had any idea how hard it would be to become a Princess and be so much in the public eye, but she didn't flinch. Once in the Royal Household there were frequent rumors about how isolated she was, how she didn't fit in, and how the Queen didn't seem to get on with her. I don't think it's worthwhile pointing fingers now, but she did suffer. Perhaps we can understand the situation more fully if we think of the newly-married Diana as an Orphan who had not been successfully adopted into the Royal Household, and partly this had to do with the existence of Camilla Parker-Bowles as Charles' mistress. Diana, as an Innocent before her wedding, clearly expected a love-marriage. When she found she'd been misled she became an Orphan, but she didn't stay in that place of despair; she did the all-but-unthinkable and divorced him.

We have only to look at Diana's transformation in those short years as she moved from being a seemingly shy and monosyllabic school-teacher who seemed to fear the press, and became the woman who knew how to use the media with consummate skill to address not just her own needs but those of her charities as well. In fact we could say that, since her image was so powerful as a factor in the public work she undertook, there really was no difference between her needs and those of her causes.

So what made this transition possible? I'd argue that Diana's inner strength as an Innocent made her able to move beyond the potential pit-falls of Orphanhood, and that she stayed an Orphan only a comparatively short time. She took all her energy – energy that she wasn't fully able to use in her marriage – and put it into her spectacularly successful charity work. She became the 'People's Princess,' famously embracing AIDS patients when the Queen and many other people would not even shake hands with them. In this way she ensured that she was accessible and compassionate in a way that the rest of the Royal Family was not. The Royal Family may not have accepted her, but Diana was determined to do things her way. Her Orphan rebelliousness gathered steam until she truly was on a course of her own. She divorced Charles because, she said, the marriage was 'a bit crowded' with a royal mistress alongside. She refused to settle for a sham marriage. This refusal, together with her decision to do things her own way, marks her as a Pilgrim who had found a set of values she was prepared to stick up for, which then allowed her to act on those values as a Warrior, in fact.

It must have taken a huge amount of courage. The press was remorseless and ready to turn on her at a moment's notice. Remarkably, though, Diana kept on doing her charity work. Her work with landmines is particularly interesting as she identified with the Innocents (mostly children) who were mutilated and killed by these devices. In this way she was taking her own sense of grief and personal injustice, which she had certainly suffered, and was turning it into a cause to help others. She did not cling to her Orphan status, although it must have been a temptation to play the pity card. She went out and had love affairs, according to the media. A lesser person would have chosen to disappear from view. She didn't, and she also seemed determined to have a personal loving relationship no matter what the public rumor-mill said. In fact one could say that Diana showed signs of being a Warrior-Lover whose public works seemed very likely to move her to Monarch level – even if she would never actually be Queen of England. Who knows where she might have found herself if she hadn't been killed in the Paris car accident?

Of course, Diana was also a person, and imperfect. Some loved her, some loathed her, and all had their reasons. If we can step back from personal preference and see the overall trajectory of her life, we can observe that she did develop spiritually in ways we might not have expected. As we think of the other Royal divorces, we can draw a few comparisons. Captain Mark Phillips married and divorced Princess Anne, and has remained a somewhat shadowy figure ever since;

certainly he does not seem to have achieved Diana's status as a public figure. Lady Sarah Ferguson married and divorced Prince Andrew, and her contributions to the public world have been similarly muted. She did a series of lectures and ads for a diet company, and that appears to be about all. If we use these two as comparisons then Princess Diana's example is all the more remarkable; she used her position for the good of many people, not just herself.

Prince Charles, in his own way, has begun to step forward more fully also in recent years. He has given lectures on architecture, promoted the charitable foundation that bears his name, and has continued to be involved in the arts, as well as promoting alternative health modalities. He has insisted on being a Prince who uses his situation to try to benefit the poor and underprivileged. Perhaps he would have done this if he had never met Diana, or perhaps her example helped him to become more forthright, possibly giving him the nudge he needed. There's no way of knowing for sure, yet it might be possible to say that even after her death Diana's example has enabled him to step forward and be more honest and open. Even though he didn't have to he did finally marry Camilla Parker-Bowles. He could have just continued the affair and avoided undue publicity. It's as if his divorce from Diana helped to create a situation that would, later, allow him to be more publicly honest. If so, there are touches of the Magician in this. I like to think that Diana, for all her mistakes, brought sufficient courage into the House of Windsor to allow for more honesty and less formal holding steady of the ranks. It's this courage that we need to think about if we are to consider what it is that creates the transition from Orphan to the next levels.

This leads us to consider Camilla, since in some ways she mirrors Charles. Her early life seems to have been such that she was deemed unsuitable to marry Charles, so she became his mistress even when married to someone else. What are we to make of this? Is this the action of a schemer? Is this fundamentally dishonest? It's hard to tell and there will be many opinions. What I think we could focus upon is that Camilla not only seems to love Charles, but she continued to do so despite both their marriages. It must have taken a great deal of arranging and determination to live like that. A lesser person would have given up entirely. It seems safe to say that Camilla may have made a mistake in her first marriage, but she didn't give up. She stayed true for many years until she was finally able to get the man she wanted. In terms of our discussion here it would be fair to say that Camilla's first marriage may have represented a giving-in to a seemingly impossible problem and a wish to make the best of a less-than-perfect situation. That is what Orphans do. They take second best because they're afraid they can't get what they want; so they conform. Charles, in marrying Diana, also did not act in harmony with his deepest desires, and neither is to be criticized for those actions. Both acted as Orphans, bowing to social pressures. What is remarkable is that Camilla decided to go her own way, acting on her own truth, and take the risks. While not as fully in the public eye as Diana she still showed signs of fighting for what she wanted as a Warrior-Lover.

We have no way of knowing how history will view her, but I can't help thinking that one of her gifts might be that she seems to have brought an understated sense of stability back to the Royal Family. She seems to get on with everyone and to be the quiet diplomat. I'm sure the Royal Family is relieved about that. Perhaps she may even bring a measure of healing to a family that has had more than its fair share of divorces and upset; for three out of four children in one family to be divorced is well above the average. Camilla may not be as obviously glamourous as Diana, but it is her quiet persistence that we may want to remember, as well as her ability to recover from the misstep of her first marriage; Camilla honored the love she shared with Charles. Diana realized her own love for Charles was not fully reciprocated and she honored love also by refusing to debase it.

If there is a lesson for us in all this it could be summed up as this: if we are to remove ourselves from Orphan lives we will need to look into our own strengths as Innocents. If we can recapture that sense of real attachment, of courage, that feeling of what is right and what is true for us, then we can power ourselves forward. One way of doing that is to love ourselves enough in order to respect our beliefs and our needs, and to love others and work for their good.

Notes

1. *Bridezillas* is produced by September Films. It first aired in 2001 and in 2004 moved to the Women's Entertainment channel, where it has been the highest rated program on the network.
2. "Lives of quiet desperation" is from Henry David Thoreau's *Walden* (1854).
3. *Desperate Housewives*, second season, 2005.
4. *Lost Boys of the Sudan: A Documentary Film*, by Megan Mylan and Jon Shenk, distributed by Actual Films and Principe Productions, 2003. The film's title is now widely used of the phenomenon of child refugees in this part of the world.
5. *The Fishing Boys of Ghana* was the title of Oprah's 2007 TV show devoted to this human trafficking situation. The name has now been adopted by the State Department. See their website: http://usinfo.State.Gov/gi/Archive/2005/Apr/19-836711.html.
6. William Faulkner quotation – widely reported. See: www.littlebluelight.com.
7. Milan Kundera, *The Book of Laughter and Forgetting*, trans. Aaron Asher, (New York: Harper Perennial, 1999).
8. The quotation is from Princess Diana's BBC TV interview, aired on ABC-TV Nov. 24. 1995. The full text of the interview, which makes fascinating reading and shows her as a lost Orphan making herself anew, can be seen at http://scoop.evansville.net/diana.html

Chapter Six

Pilgrim Love

The Pilgrim is the person who opts to move away from the consoling comforts of a settled existence and asks questions about what more there might be to discover in the world, or in herself. This can be tumultuous, like Gauguin's departure for Tahiti, but it does not have to be. Two Orphans who love each other may find that as their love grows they want to connect more to the spiritual meanings they feel drawn to explore, and, moved by the wonder of what they feel, they become Pilgrims. If only one partner feels this way we have the danger of an unbalanced relationship. We've all seen these. Stereotypically the woman wants more depth and the man wants things to remain the same.

This brings us to one of the main dangers of the Pilgrim phase, which is that Pilgrims can always slip back to being Orphans. That's their great temptation – to give up their search for meaning. They can opt for the safe-bet, perhaps because they're tired of unsatisfactory relationships, or because they feel they're getting old and the biological clock is ticking, or because they don't believe real love is out there for them. Some become discouraged with their partners and have children anyway, and they look to those children to provide the love and sense of meaning they crave. This can be dangerous ground. The over-involved parent can do as much damage as any influence I can think of. In their neediness the unspoken requirement is that the child should in some ways complete them, or justify their existence. And yet no one's task in life is to live *for* another person. No one can "complete" anyone else. That is their own work, and theirs alone.

To understand the Pilgrim we need to look back for a moment to the Orphan. Orphans are the people who are most likely to believe that someone else can make them better than they presently are. This is the old daydream of 'one day my prince will come.' It suggests that all one has to do is sit around, waiting, and then the miracles will occur. It's an easy, even a lazy option, based upon not believing one has any agency in one's own life. In my counseling work I've come across many people who have slipped into this way of thinking. And yet even Cinderella didn't sit around and do nothing; she mobilized the slender resources she had and she went to the ball to make sure she met the prince, and she did so not once but three times. Even Cinderella had to get up out of the dust and cinders, fabricate her dress and coach (with a little help, of course) and venture out into the world as a Pilgrim. She knew she was an Orphan – her stepmother and stepsisters constantly reminded her of that – and she also knew that unless she took action nothing could change. In some versions of the legend the creatures she has been kind to help Cinderella – the birds help her sort out the lentils her stepmother has poured into the ashes for example. In another version the mice she spares from the traps become her coach horses. This little detail is emblematic of what happens for the Pilgrims of the world: they may be on a search for meaning but they still need to be kind to others, and this kindness will serve them well. In fact in the tale Cinderella is frequently seen with birds and animals, which suggests that she is somehow in touch with the vital and instinctual part of herself. If we see things in this way then the white bird (the fairy godmother of later versions) is not a creature who appears merely to solve the problems; it is an emblem of the Pilgrim's ability to think differently. In this fairy tale Cinderella really wanted to go to the ball, and she wouldn't be put off.

The Pilgrim's life is rarely easy, since even though she goes out boldly into the world looking for real attachment, she can also get lost in what looks like emotional exploration but is in fact merely the exchange of partners, or friends, or jobs, on a regular basis. A true Pilgrim is on a path that will lead, she hopes, to a meaningful relationship with another person, one that will allow each person to achieve further growth as the relationship continues. But many people are afraid of that. A comparison here might be with shopping for a car. Most people choose the car that suits their needs, now. They gauge it so that they know roughly how much it's likely to cost. Then they work out monthly payments so there are no surprises. Now imagine if you bought a car, which then began to grow, develop, change, take up more space, demand more time … and it might, just might, become something more than a car. It's a bit scary, yet that is what the Pilgrim wants. The sense of purpose that comes with that love is for the Pilgrim absolutely central. Love has to be able to grow.

If we return to *Cinderella* for a second, what we can see is that Cinderella has to go to the ball on three occasions. She takes her chances and she doesn't give up at the first attempt. In a very real way she is demonstrating to herself and others what she could be if she were to become the Prince's spouse. She has ventured well beyond her usual limits, yet she seems to be aware that she can't just stay at the ball and have everything work out miraculously, at least not at that moment. Her leaving at midnight is symbolic of the point at which one day ends and another begins: she is a creature on the point of change, yet she cannot be changed into the

Princess permanently until the Prince moves out of his preferred comfort zone as well. He is the one who declares he will track down and find this mysterious girl. He could just give up. Instead he takes risks. After all, he is the one who gets fooled twice by the wicked sisters who cut off toes in order to get their feet into the tiny slipper. What a wonderful image that is of what some Orphans will do in order to 'fit in'! They will literally destroy parts of themselves – even cripple themselves – to get what they think everyone will envy them for. In our world of cosmetic surgery this is surely not such an alien concept, although worse than this are those people who limit their mental attitudes and act dumb in order to gain approval.

While this is going on the Prince is, in his own fashion, becoming a Pilgrim as well. He goes out looking for the woman who has enchanted him, and he stands by his word. Notice that the ugly sisters are still just as ugly as before and surely everyone has noticed this, but the Prince has said he will marry the person whose foot fits the slipper, and he stands by what he has declared. Interestingly, in the Grimm brothers' original rendition of this tale the sisters were actually beautiful, but had wicked hearts, which makes the Prince's task a little different and a little more difficult. Even so, he must have noticed that the sister he carries off on each occasion is not the same as Cinderella, but he agrees to honor his promise. This is a man who can be trusted to keep his word. He's also a fine representative of the Pilgrim and what the Pilgrim occasionally has to do, which is to stick to his course even though it looks to be horribly mistaken. In some versions of the story when the Prince sees the ugly sisters' bleeding feet he becomes so enraged at their attempts to deceive him that he orders them whipped. In the Grimm brothers' version doves come and peck out the sisters' eyes. Doves are emblematic of peace, and turtle doves are symbols of eternal fidelity. It is as if even nature is appalled at the deceptions the sisters have perpetrated, which are bound to lead to unhappiness. One cannot help thinking that a strong action, such as pecking out the eyes, is part of the story's inner logic that seeks to show that Pilgrims must have an absolute respect for the truth *and they demand it from others*. Appearances are not enough, hence the detail of the eyes. The Pilgrim searches for real love, and the Warrior-Lover refuses to compromise.

It's only when both Cinderella and her Prince have gone through three attempts to find each other that the story can come to a happy conclusion. And here we must not overlook the nature of the story's ending. It's not just that Cinderella gets a promotion and becomes a Princess; it's more a case of the rich and worldly Prince – obviously a male, authoritarian figure used to dispensing justice – who is united with his female counterpart, who is gentle and caring. Remember, the mice and rats that become Cinderella's coachmen and horses were actually saved by her from the traps around the kitchen, which seems to show a tender heart, and the doves of the Grimm version are as we have seen symbolic of peace and harmony. This uniting of 'male' power with the 'female' attribute of compassion allows for the symbolic uniting of the Warrior with the Lover as the couple marries and becomes in the eyes of the church one flesh, and in the eyes of the world a true Monarch Pairing.

This brief run through of the fairy tale is here to emphasize that the Pilgrim's struggle is never simply a vague wandering from place to place. It is something that is deeply demanding, sometimes plagued with missteps, and always requires courage. We can imagine what the King would have thought of his son bringing home a penniless kitchen drudge, yet the Prince knows that he and Cinderella together can transcend those obvious objections. The inner qualities are what matter, not the outer attributes so beloved of Orphans.

This brings us to one important detail. Cinderella gets her name because she has been relegated to sit in the ashes and tend the fire. She's an Orphan – the wicked stepmother reminds her of that – who seems to be reduced to mere drudgery as a slave. Yet her time sitting in the ashes can be seen as a metaphor that shows an inner growth, a time of mourning for what is lost that she knows how to throw aside when the right time comes. Pilgrims often have to spend time mulling over who they are, and sometimes rejection and humiliation provide the necessary impetus. Most of us don't do deep soul work when everything's going just fine; sometimes a reversal of fortune is what we need to spur us forward.

The Challenges of the Pilgrim: The Pilgrim Trap

Obviously, being a Pilgrim can be hard work. People recognize the independent aspect of the Pilgrim and are attracted to it. They also see that the Pilgrim hasn't found what he or she needs yet, and so is somewhat unpredictable and therefore a risky bet. What tends to happen is that people who have many excellent qualities, but who happen to be Orphans at heart, may try to "tame" the Pilgrim, or to "save" him or her. This is entirely in tune with the Orphan's world view. It's much safer and cozier to be back in the predictable world of established values. Orphans love having Pilgrims around them because their restlessness offers a whiff of glamor without the necessity of joining the struggle personally. Many hearts are broken when Orphans and Pilgrims get together. Sometimes the Orphan plays the "rescue me" card, and the Pilgrim falls for this play, feeling a temporary sense of power and direction in setting someone else right. But the Pilgrim quickly feels trapped in the dependence he or she has encouraged, because what any Pilgrim really needs is to be free of people wanting him or her to be a certain way. Pilgrims feel they want to be their *own* way.

And so Pilgrims have been accused of being heartless, of being cold, of being selfish, rejecting, or "lost." Just look at Cinderella's angry Prince, sentencing the ugly sisters to ferocious punishments. How cruel! Yet he has to reject, and forcibly reject, what is not right. And here is where we have to be aware of a potential trap that lies in wait for the Pilgrim: sometimes the Pilgrim looks to reject others since that is the only way to continue the search and remain as a Pilgrim. Accepting love may lead the Pilgrim to have to come to Warrior-Lover status, and this may seem more than is manageable. Ultimately this is because the Pilgrim does not yet love herself sufficiently to be able to make that leap. The Pilgrim trap lies in becoming more devoted to the habit of being a Pilgrim than seeing it as a stage that must be moved through. Whenever anyone becomes more attached to the form of an activity than to what the activity is leading to, then that person has accepted a formula for life and has turned away from life itself. Living by a formula is what the Orphan does. And so the person who seems at first sight to be the perpetual searcher is, in some cases, just another version of the Orphan. It is very easy for any of us, therefore, to slip back in this way.

So what keeps the Pilgrim on course?

Simply put, the Pilgrim has to find a purpose in *life* as well as a purpose in *love,* and that is the difference. An Orphan can accept others' definitions of what life is about, or even accept that life isn't about very much at all except moving ahead, getting promoted, and moving to a larger place as the years roll by. The Pilgrim has to have a belief that she has come to for herself, in her own time, and *then* will seek to be with other like-minded souls.

The Pilgrim learns about love and attachment by seeking after a cause, an idea, a sense of purposeful activity. I think that is what lies behind so many of the people who decide to pursue their career first, and then find a partner. The Pilgrim has to want whatever it is she wants not because of the gratification of applause (that's the Orphan's reward) but because doing the task is in some senses its own reward. I have met writers who have said they'd be writing even if they didn't get published because it's what they love to do, and they feel it brings them closer to something true. And I've also met artists who have freely confessed that the only thing that kept them working was the money, and they'd give it up to-morrow if they could. It's not what you do, it's the spirit you bring to what you do that makes the difference.

Returning to *Cinderella*, then, there are more observations we can make. At the start of the tale (according to the Grimm brothers' version) Cinderella's father goes on a trip and asks what he can bring back. The two stepsisters ask for expensive dresses. Cinderella asks for a sprig of the first tree that knocks against her father's hat. This is surely a bizarre request and it begs to be decoded. The sisters want to look good, and so they act according to that Orphan thinking. Cinderella's request produces a hazel twig, which she plants on her mother's grave, and which grows into a tree that will later provide her with her dresses on the three days of the ball. The twig that knocks against her father's hat is emblematic of nature removing (or nearly removing) his symbol of authority – his hat. Hats were routinely seen as marks of rank, which was why people removed them in the presence of those who were of higher rank, and why hats were sometimes so elaborate. The armed services still have far more glamorous hats for their higher ranking officers than for lower ranks. So we can see the request for the twig as Cinderella's awareness that she is in tune with natural growth and maturation rather than with issues of authority, and it is her honoring of that natural process that is evident when she plants the twig on her mother's grave. The tree resulting from this planting returns her compliment, and gives her the dresses she needs, which hang in its branches almost like fruit which appear when the time is right. Notice how often Cinderella is linked to natural things – the hazel tree, the birds who help her sort out the seeds, the doves who punish the step-sisters, and now ripe fruit. The tale seems to show that whatever we think is happening to this girl, she is undergoing a process that is natural and maturational. Notice also how she has no doubt at all that she should go to the ball. She does not accept her step-mother's veto. She knows she has to be there, just as the prince knows he now has to be married. This is the Pilgrim's sense of knowing – that inner certainty that, if we trust it, will lead us where we need to go. This brings us back to that hazel twig. She plants it on her mother's grave, and it becomes an emblem of how Cinderella is able to feel the strength of her mother's love even though her mother is long dead. Cherishing that love lets her know that despite anything her step-mother says she is lovable, and that leads her to trust implicitly her own judgment. The story suggests that without that basic mother-love Cinderella would not have the core of belief necessary to grow emotionally. She finds her strength through being able to contact the Innocent within.

The question then arises as to why Cinderella flees the prince at the end of each night's dancing. In terms of plot this allows him to come looking for her, as we have seen, and so allows him to be a Pilgrim and a Warrior-Lover. In terms of psychology it represents the need of the Pilgrim who has newly become a Warrior-Lover to declare herself – and it shows how tempting it can be to retreat from that to the familiar drudgery of being an Orphan. That's what Cinderella does, and it's also a familiar pattern we see in other folk tales (*Iron John*, for example) when the hero steps forward and takes action and then steps back on three occasions. It signals to us that most of us cannot make this bold transition to Warrior-Lover unless we have been able to create a compelling attachment to another first, and that other person will have to accept us for who we are becoming rather than for who we once were.

This is important. I've come across couples who have argued and bitterly reproached each other with facts about their past history, or place of birth. To say that someone is "trash from the wrong side of the tracks," as one young woman reported her significant other had said, is not helpful. Anyone can be born poor, and no one gets to choose exactly where he or she takes that first breath. To reproach one's partner with history is like racism, since no one can change the past or the color of one's skin. We can, of course, all change how we are in the present moment; we can look at our lover knowing that each of us has had some less than admirable experiences and not hold that in any way against that person. What matters for Cinderella is the rapport she has with her Prince when she dances with him, when she becomes his preferred partner. It's not where you come from but who you become when you are with the person you love that matters.

Armed with this knowledge we can now say that the difference between Pilgrim and Orphan stages is one of intent rather than degree. An Orphan can be ferociously attached to a person he or she hardly knows, or to a philosophy that has not been properly thought out. Political extremists have exploited this human need mercilessly. Orphans attach because they are terrified of being unattached. Pilgrims want attachment but are questioners, sometimes rejecters, and so they seem at first glance to be difficult souls who reject other perfectly good people.

"I can't believe he won't respond to her. She loves him so much." That's the way one woman described the situation she observed, and, without oversimplifying I think we can see an Orphan mentality judging an Orphan-Pilgrim mismatch. "I just want someone to love me," declared another person – voicing a primary need we all have, and yet doing so in an uncritical way. This could be the cry of the Orphan in the dark night. The Pilgrim wants love just as much, but has to be sure the offered love is a good match that will not derail the search for the soul. For that is what the Pilgrim is doing.

Put another way the Orphan is looking for the consolations of the ego. As we've already seen it is the ego that tells us that we are who we are because of how others see us. We have our identity to some extent as a result of the things we have, the sort of friends we have, and the job we have. Losing the good regard of others is hugely painful to the Orphan ego.

The Pilgrim trusts the ego less because she has found its rewards to be unsatisfying. She knows that she is more than her possessions because she feels them to be not enough, somehow. In these circumstances the emerging Pilgrim can get way-laid by addictions. Addiction can, at first, let one fit in. The tortured teen who becomes more fun when drunk is, in the conventional phrase, self-medicating, and the medicating is designed to *lessen* the pain of not fitting in. You see the pattern: after a while addictions become an identity in themselves. The search for money to feed a habit, the prowl for the fix – these give the ego a purpose at the same time as they offer the illusion of transcending the ego. This kind of Orphan thinking – attachment to the addiction – thus swamps the emerging Pilgrim while seeming to offer the opposite. No wonder it's so hard to break addictions.

I have limited experience working with addicts, but it seems to me from the people I have worked with that addictions and compulsive behaviors can be shaken when the individual develops the ability to stand aside from the ego and observe the situation from the outside. The "observing ego" is what asks us awkward questions. We're told we should want certain things in life. The observing ego is not merely reactive. It does not just scream, "Yes!" and go for the socially accepted behaviors. The observing ego asks: "So, why do I feel this won't do it for me?" This takes courage. To ask, "Is that all there is?" can be an alarming question and to try to find an answer can be downright terrifying, especially as everyone else seems happy doing what they all agree is good. If we consider addictions, rarely does someone sit up one day and say, "I'm going to abuse alcohol" or whatever the drug of choice happens to be. Addictions are almost always social. The sampling action happens because it seems to be the accepted thing to do in that particular clique at that particular time for that designated purpose. Depressed? Take a drink and forget about it! That's Orphan thinking. Yet the person who has an observing (and observant) ego is unlikely to find this a real remedy. Orphans do what everyone else does, even if it doesn't really work. Pilgrims are likely to have the courage of their own opinions, which is a form of self-love.

So, where does that self-love come from that makes Pilgrims able to refuse Orphan-thinking and why doesn't everyone have it? I suggest we all have that self-love, but it can get crushed out of us by Orphan culture. We loved and respected ourselves as Innocents. Somewhere that powerful sense of self is undermined, and it may well be because in mass cultures such as ours it is harder to stand up against group-think than it ever was before. Mass culture is a relatively new phenomenon. Prior to about 1750 in the Western world it didn't exist, and people conformed in a general fashion since conforming was, really, about survival. It would be marvelous to be able to construct a sense of a lost golden age in which people were encouraged to find themselves as fully as possible, but seductive as this is, it's hardly likely to be true. Society has always depended upon people being predictable, and this has since become increasingly true. For example, today our society in the U.S. demands ever more years of schooling of its potential middle-class employees. The prevailing thought is that anyone who really wants to get and keep a decent job with prospects and medical benefits has to complete 12 grades of school, and 5 years (the national average) of a Bachelor's degree. We could add to that a further 2 years for a Master's degree, plus various training seminars for our teachers, medical professionals and upper level managers. Whether one considers this lengthy process efficient or a huge unnecessary investment in a social institution matters less than that a new MA graduate, at age 28, has spent perhaps 19 or 20 of those years being schooled. Inevitably such people learn to conform as much or more than people in other, earlier societies would have done under pressures delivered by church or government. Any student who has loans to pay off will confirm that she simply has to fit in and earn the money to pay back her obligations. It's not an option for most people to emerge from their education and be able to experiment with their career possibilities. Debt forces many of us into Orphan status right away.

Perhaps all one can say is that those who choose to question the accepted order have usually been in the minority, and that in itself could be one reason that after all these millennia of human history we're all still confused about who we should be, let alone what Love might be. Not enough people have questioned the accepted order with courage and determination.

Points to Ponder:
Rejection as a Way of Life

The Pilgrim can seem contrary, rejecting, cold, and lost; as we've seen what is really going on is an in-depth search for meaning. The Pilgrim may look, longingly, for love and then feel she has to reject it, or test it so much that the partner is tempted to give up. This can be torture for all concerned. Sometimes the Pilgrim simply seems angry at the world, since she's looking for deeper values and can't seem to find them fast enough.

People will tend to want to "sort out" the Pilgrim, by making her into an adopted Orphan. Men often seem to want to "tame" strong individualistic women, for example, and women urge men to "settle down." Yet a real Pilgrim will always yearn for spiritual growth.

An example of this desire to 'tame' is perhaps what happens when police or authoritarian forces attempt to restrain angry protesters. When discontented people meet those who wish to silence them, as they see it, there may even be serious pitched battles. Each side is reacting to the other in a predictable way. And so we could say that the represser helps to create the protester just as the protester helps to create the repressive reaction. There's really no difference between them. This is an example of how easily the Pilgrim, with all her questioning courage at her disposal, can be sucked into a mere adversarial stance that ensures a stalemate. It may seem to be a Warrior-Lover action, but in fact it isn't. The Pilgrim who gets caught in this dance is much more likely to slip back into Orphan stage, demonizing the opposition, plotting against them, and accepting rebel orthodoxy. What a pity! After all, the point about meeting with the powers of conflicting authority is not to fight with them; that's simply playing at their own game, and one that they are very good at. The point is to persuade them to do otherwise than they have been doing, to encourage them to think. Gandhi's strategy of non-violence was about exactly that; it really did make people question what they were doing, and why.

Consider that example brought to a more domestic level. The young woman who is urged to marry the rising executive by her controlling parents, though she feels no real affinity for the young man, would be right to feel angry, trapped and upset. In one case I came across the woman felt that everyone wanted her to marry the accountant boyfriend, even though she felt he was not truly committed to personal growth to the extent she needed. She tried hard to get him to see things her way, and he tried equally hard to respect her point of view while sticking to his own sense of what was important. The confrontations became less and less loving and when they parted the woman, in reaction, began a series of affairs with people who were clearly not her intellectual equals. She saw conventional society and the desire for wealth as her enemies. Several years later she had a child with a man from Tibet with whom she did not even have a language in common, and when she became pregnant with a second child, she discovered that he was just as controlling as the situations she thought she had left behind. He would not let her leave. He threatened her. Eventually she managed to flee with her children. And suddenly she was back home, being supported by her parents, battling them and their attitudes at every turn.

It's a sad scenario. So what happened? I think one could say that the woman was an emerging Pilgrim who made the mistake of defining herself, after a major disappointment in love, as someone who was in opposition to others. Once she had chosen that role she felt she had to live it; and whenever we live in reaction to others, or to our perception of others, we tend to stop thinking. That's when we can slip back into Orphanhood. That is what this young woman did, literally, as she became dependent on her family once again. With the drama she had created around herself, and with two young children to take care of, she had no time to stand outside her situation and ask how it had come to be that way. She regarded herself as a 'failure' rather than being able to view herself as a Pilgrim who was temporarily off course, and so she became embittered. She attached to her mistakes, and the seemingly hopeless nature of her situation. With that mind set it is very hard to become a Pilgrim again, since being a Pilgrim is always an act of optimism, and never an act of surrender.

I hope – I expect – that this woman will find her way back to Pilgrim status and be able to move beyond it. For the moment, though, there are considerable obstacles for her to overcome. She will need to access that observing ego again so that she can see herself and her situation anew.

Pilgrims can interrupt their pilgrimages for years in just this way, especially when raising children. Some – a few – manage to pursue their pilgrimage by observing their spiritual growth *as parents*. This is very hard for those who have jobs and mortgage payments, or who are living from inadequate paycheck to inadequate paycheck and are attempting to feed and clothe children at the same time.

So we can see that the restless Pilgrim can be bad news, at least for a while. The parent who is an unreconciled Pilgrim can do huge amounts of damage if she allows her frustrations to spill out into her childrearing in an uncontrolled way. An angry, depressed, unfulfilled, and resentful parent is modeling conflict and children are sensitive to the ways parents treat *themselves*. They see it and then do the same thing to their own psyches.

In the Bedroom:
The Restless Spirit

The Pilgrim can be, in some ways, the most anxious of lovers, since she knows she is on a quest – even if she's not sure what the quest is yet – and so is troubled by uncertainty. Is this the person I really want to be with? Is this the physical relationship I want? What if I'm making a mistake? What if there's somebody better? These sorts of doubts may be healthy, but they tend to have an inhibiting effect on the free, unrestrained playfulness that is sex at its most expressive and fulfilling. The Pilgrim may seem sexually adventurous, yet this may be because as a Pilgrim she wants to try out new possibilities, new positions, new toys, in case she's missing out on something. While this can be fun, the important thing is not what one does but the spirit in which one does it. Sexual experimentation can be rewarding and pleasurable, but not if it involves betraying one's partner, for example, or treating the other person's attachment as disposable.

Sometimes the Pilgrim can be so much in her own thoughts that sex doesn't happen at all, or is perfunctory. When this occurs we occasionally see an internal contradiction acted out because the Pilgrim yearns for a passionate attachment that she cannot as yet believe in, and so she will have to will herself into a state of loving sexuality. When one is young and the hormones are raging this is not hard to achieve, of course, and so the Pilgrim has a real responsibility to listen to herself honestly or risk causing extensive pain for herself and others. Especially for women

Pilgrims it may be difficult to feel pleasure in sex, and they may find orgasm hard to achieve. This is, in most cases, because the woman does not feel a convincing connection to her partner, and so cannot relax enough to enjoy love and sex.

Historically the Pilgrim was expected to remain celibate throughout the pilgrimage, and indeed some people in Pilgrim stage elect to give up sex. As one woman put it: "I wasn't going to have sex and get a partner just for the sake of not being lonely. I was either going to find someone I could truly love or I'd live like a nun." This is when the individual starts to understand the difference between libido and real desire. Libido – basic sexual appetite – begins to feel unsatisfactory unless it can be tied to some deeper sense of emotional connection. This is hard for the Pilgrim since she hasn't yet defined what her personal values might be, and so connection is something she regards with suspicion. Two Pilgrims may both be seeking a soul connection when they meet, but they may well have differing senses of what they think they might need, and so they will tend not to trust what they feel. Sometimes this sort of struggle is fought out over issues such as where each person wishes to place energy or personal resources. An example would be that perhaps one wants to buys a house and the other isn't sure which city her career may take her to and so opposes any purchase or quietly sabotages the process. The outer struggle may be about the house, yet it is also a metaphor in which each partner is trying to choose where to invest the full amount of his or her love. Both may desire to grow and to explore aspects of themselves in their relationship, but each can end up perceiving the other as a stumbling block. At the very moment when they are more similar to each other than ever, they may decide to part.

By contrast, for the Orphan pleasure is the main object, and whatever gives pleasure is most valued. The unbalanced Orphan, of course, only thinks of physical pleasure, and so can become confused easily about what makes for a strong relationship. The balanced Orphan seeks physical combined with emotional pleasure, and it is quite possible for two Orphans to find this. Two balanced Orphans can feel themselves to be adequately connected, although they may not be connected in the truly vital way the Pilgrim yearns for. They may 'get on' well, and seem contented. The Pilgrim, though, begins to demand more. Libido, and the simple desire for sex, becomes unsatisfactory because it appears to be separated from a real, equal, emotional connection. This dissatisfaction won't be resolved until the Pilgrim becomes a Warrior-Lover.

Exploring the Energy of the Archetype

To contact and explore the energy of the Pilgrim and feel it fully we may need to think about what it feels like to be on a journey. The Pilgrim is a traveler who wants to get to a destination. Can you think of a time when you set out on a journey that had a successful conclusion? What did you take? Was it hard to pack? Did you find yourself taking too much or too little? How did you decide what to include? Think about that for a moment. Draw up a list. To some extent the things we take with us are going to represent the values we hold close, values we expect to have endorsed by the experience. If you take party clothes it's likely to mean you want to develop that part of yourself and that social fun is an important value you're going to explore. If you took hiking gear it would indicate a desire for a different type of experience. Sometimes people go on a trip or vacation and come back saying: 'I want more of that in my life!' Sometimes they say the exact opposite. They've learned something about themselves in each case. Every trip has some aspect of a pilgrimage in it. What can you learn from yours?

When thinking about your travels ask yourself also how you dealt with any upsets along the way. One of the best ways to access the energy of the Pilgrim is to focus on a trip that involved some physical demands upon you. How did you feel walking up that hillside? How did it feel when you got to the top of the mountain? How did you deal with those who said your projected route was silly? Whether it's a twenty mile walk up a mountain peak, a road trip that took three days, or the search for the thing you really wanted in an antiques fair, it makes little difference. The point is that you took on obstacles and you did things your own way.

Some people remind themselves of this energy by having pictures of themselves on lofty mountain tops, or snapshots of them taking part in marathons, triathlons, canoe trips, holding up large fish, or whatever. Some have maps on their walls, others have souvenirs of outlandish places. One man I worked with had a small tortoise shell strung on beads that he traded with a Kalahari bushman for an old tweed jacket, miles from anywhere in the desert. I have a tattered and grubby guidebook to India on my bookshelf; each time I touch it and open the pages I'm reminded of that three-month trip and I reconnect with the determination and the energy of the Pilgrim inside me. I recall the dreadful poverty I witnessed, the exhausting trips in third class railcars in mind-numbing heat, and the extraordinary temples and works of art; all these things challenged me to reflect on who I thought I was – and it wasn't always a comfortable experience.

We can only feel this energy, though, when we allow ourselves the space and time to recall the experience in detail. We may need to meditate on it. Sometimes trying to explain our motivations to someone else can be useful, too, especially when we're greeted with, "Why ever would anyone want to do *that*?" What's important is to feel the energy and enjoy it.

The Pilgrim in the Tarot

The card for the Pilgrim is also known as The Hermit, which is not a good sign for anyone who wants an intimate relationship with those who are living this archetype! The image itself is a warning. The Hermit is often depicted carrying a lamp, and this is frequently interpreted to mean that he is looking for inward illumination. It can also be seen as the limitations of walking by night when one can only see a very few steps ahead, which is another powerful image of the way the Pilgrim has to function without a fully developed long-range plan. Again, the Hermit is sometimes depicted wearing a monk's hood and gown, and this, as with all details in the Tarot, is not accidental. The Hermit can be 'hooded', concealing her real identity (think of Cinderella) and also

THE HERMIT.

limited in her ability to see the whole picture, for she cannot easily look from side to side. The simplicity of the monk's habit indicates a concentration on inner riches, not display. Real pilgrims are unlikely to care much about clothes. It's also worth noting that the Hermit is walking. No horses or carriages here! Other figures in the Tarot have chariots and steeds, but the Pilgrim has to do the real footwork for herself. There are no short cuts – she has to look into things herself first hand.

Notice that a hermit may not be on a physical pilgrimage of any sort. Even so the contemplative life always involves an inner journey and therefore this figure is in the process of spiritual exploration. We can be Pilgrims without leaving our neighborhoods physically.

The Hermit card is one of very few that depicts a night scene. While the Pilgrim is searching, thinking, questioning, she is unable to see what would be plain in the full light of day. She's not yet illuminated her path fully; and just as one can feel more alone, more fragile, and less sure when in darkness, that's what life feels like for the Pilgrim. The Pilgrim therefore has to learn to rely on her inner sense of strength – just as Cinderella does. That's possibly why the Pilgrim is depicted with a staff, since she's not yet strong enough to do without it. This is signaled to us in another way, also, because the very next card up the deck is the card 'Strength', number eight. The hint seems clear: when she can access her strength of spirit the Pilgrim can transform herself into the Warrior-Lover.

You'll have noticed that so far with these images we have been moving through the Tarot from the high numbered cards towards the lower numbers, in sequence, moving 'up' the values. This will continue to be the case. And that is another factor that suggests that the Tarot is a more complex version of the six archetypes, broken into individual figures, their opposites, and the qualities they have to come to terms with as they grow. The basic ideas, though, are essential the same.

Examples in Real Life and in the Movies

In our everyday world it can be difficult to identify Pilgrims because they aren't always doing things that obviously mark them out as undergoing change. Bill Gates was for many years simply a very wealthy businessman until, at a certain point, he began his charitable works. He was truly a Monarch in the business world, but when he started using his extra money to help eradicate malaria, for example, he transitioned into a man who had found a public cause to fight for. He may have looked like a pillar of industry, but he was in fact a Pilgrim, working out how to use his talents to benefit others. Since he was already such a well-connected and high profile individual, he was able to make his impact very forcefully in short order. Once he settled on his mission it was therefore easier for him to achieve Monarch level. His experience reminds us that even though a person may be wildly successful this may not be the full weight of what he or she can achieve. Bono from U2 was in the same situation. He was tremendously successful in one area of life before he decided to use his position and leverage it into helping the very poorest of the poor. As a successful rock star he was working within the confines expected of an entertainer; when he became a philanthropist he remade the situation radically and he reached out beyond the usual geographical and cultural boundaries.

It's worth watching high profile people like these to see if they do move out of their comfort zones. I keep hoping that Paris Hilton will become more than she presently is. When she was sentenced to jail – where she served a few days rather than a few weeks – I wondered if she would begin to step outside herself and think differently. This was her descent into the ashes, so to speak. There was a flutter of excitement in the press when it was reported she'd 'found God.' So far it seems to have been wishful thinking; she doesn't appear to have reached Pilgrim level yet.

Movies frequently have examples like these. Think of Kevin Costner's *Dances with Wolves*, which won seven Academy awards. Costner plays Lt. John Dunbar, a Civil War army officer who is about to have his wounded leg amputated. Rather than submit to this, he mounts his horse and rides between the opposing lines, hoping to be killed. His ride provokes a shoot-out that breaks the stalemate and the Union soldiers win the subsequent battle. Costner is greeted as a hero, gets proper medical treatment from the General's own doctor, and is given the posting he asks for. He asks to go to the Dakota frontier. He may be a hero in name, but it's by pure accident, and when he arrives at the deserted fort he is surely an Orphan. While he is there he makes friends with the local Sioux Indians until gradually he becomes more attached to them than to the army. All this time he has, in fact, been a Pilgrim, looking for something to believe in, and he finds this in his respect for the Sioux. When he marries Stands Like a Fist (who is European but has been brought up as an adopted Sioux) he is declaring his allegiance not just to the Sioux but also to all that is loving and best in human beings regardless of their race or identity. He becomes a true Warrior-Lover and he is in marked contrast now to the less than heroic soldiers who are out to punish him as a deserter. He withdraws from the fight and from the tribe because he recognizes it as the best hope they have for peace.

Pilgrims may be all around us and we don't recognize them since they are in a state of becoming rather than in a state of being. Sometimes they don't even know it themselves. Costner's character thinks he's just being curious whereas he's actually remaking his whole moral life. His notebook, in which he carefully records the ways of the Sioux, is just the most evident sign that he is truly an explorer and investigator, one who seeks understanding. As he observes others he also reassesses himself.

Notes

1. *Cinderella* has been told in many forms. The most useful text is in *The Complete Grimm's Fairy Tales*, op. cit., tale #21, pp. 121-128.
2. *Iron John*, ibid. # 136, pp. 612-620. See also Bly, Robert. *Iron John: A Book About Men* (New York: Addison-Wesley, 2004).
3. *Dances With Wolves*, directed by Kevin Costner, 1990.

Chapter Seven

The Warrior-Lover

_____ ⌀ ⌀ _____

The Warrior-Lover is most easily described as the stage at which one decides what to fight for – since one can only fight whole-heartedly for what one truly loves, and one can only love something, or someone, fully if that person is worth fighting for.

One of the earliest descriptions of the Warrior-Lover is in Sophocles' play *Antigone*. This ancient play has echoed down the centuries and has been re-written a number of times in the process. It's clear that it articulates something important for generation after generation, and that the theme of standing up against tyranny for what one believes is right will never go out of fashion.

Antigone appears on stage already knowing she has an impossible situation ahead of her. She must bury the body of her dead brother or risk the wrath of the gods who demand that family members bury their dead. If she does so, however, she runs the risk of being sentenced to death by the king, Creon, whose enemy her brother was. Antigone does not complain or protest against the gods. She has already made up her mind what she has to do because it is right, not because it is legal. She prefers to face the anger of a king rather than offend the gods. The situation is doubly complicated because she is betrothed to Haemon, Creon's son, and she must sacrifice her own wedding plans if she decides to go against Creon. As a literal orphan, Antigone could adopt the Orphan's role and just accept what her future father-in-law decrees; but she'd have to give up her sense of what is morally right to do that.

We can't help but notice Antigone's devotion to what is right according to the highest standards, and when we discover that Haemon supports her in her moral choice we can see that she is in a relationship that is loving, supportive, and courageous. Sophocles signals to us that the Warrior-Lover must be a balance of strength and loving kindness, male and female within him or her self, and that this balance in no way makes the archetype soft or indecisive. Creon is too vain to be able to listen to Antigone's reasons or the objections of his own son, choosing instead to feel personally affronted by someone whom he thinks does not respect him as king. His vindictiveness marks him as a mean-spirited person, an Orphan who hides behind his title. He orders Antigone to be walled up alive – another sort of burial. The Creons of this world are always trying to stifle dissent. Horrified by this punishment, Croen's son rushes to the vault and arrives just too late to prevent Antigone from hanging herself, and then he too kills himself after coming close to killing Creon. Creon loses his son and his future daughter-in-law – and thus his dynastic hopes – whereupon his wife kills herself and completes his isolation.

The tale can be seen as the confrontation of principled-living with vanity, and it can also be seen as what happens when the Warrior-Lover archetype is not permitted its freedom. The result is a blighted succession. Antigone and Haemon are balanced as male and female, and neither lacks for courage or resolution, which shows them as each balanced in themselves. Both of them argue with Creon respectfully but with force, urging compassion and some flexibility, and Creon comes off as looking very petty since he prefers to have his revenge on the already decaying corpse rather than considering what the situation is right there and then for the living people concerned.

Although Antigone does not succeed in the triumphant way so beloved of Hollywood, hers is a bracing, magnificent failure that leaves us recognizing the power of example even if it does not win through. Antigone's name has since become a byword for courage in our culture. One can love one's partner, and yet still have to do what is ultimately right.

To understand further the challenges faced by the Warrior-Lover we can also look at the case of Oedipus.

In the play *Oedipus Rex*, Oedipus is an Orphan who takes to the road as a Pilgrim. Since the prophecy says he'll kill his father and marry his mother, he wants desperately to avoid that. A passive Orphan might just shrug and accept this fate. Oedipus is repelled by it and runs away to find a life that is truly his own – true Pilgrim motivations. At a place where three roads converge he meets his unknown birth father, gets into a conflict, and kills him. He then goes on to marry his mother, the dead man's widow.

The key phrase is "where three roads meet." Three roads offer three choices – go back, or take one of the forks. Oedipus takes the fork that leads to violence. His unknown father, King Laius, is the one who starts the fight – he tries to whip Oedipus out of the way – but was it really necessary to kill him and his attendants? Laius was a king and kings are often rather full of themselves. Oedipus' response is one of personal, ego-based affront. 'No one treats *me* that way,' he seems to say. He enters the realm of the Warrior but not the realm of the Lover, and by taking on violence he fuels his own sense of pride rather than reaching for any understanding. So Oedipus becomes a pseudo-Warrior and, since he really does kill his biological father in this encounter, he unknowingly becomes an actual Orphan.

There are plenty of people who, like Oedipus, think that decisive, violent, ego-based actions make them Warrior-Lovers, when in fact such choices have missed the mark entirely and lead only to Orphanhood. Public figures tend to be the most obvious examples of this. Donald Trump in that strange TV show *The Apprentice* takes on the role of the all-powerful business mogul who fires people at the least provocation, but he's hardly the most successful of businessmen himself and he comes across as a rather shallow poseur. The show is a ghastly parody of real business practices; I mention it because so many people, it seems, think it is accurate. Presumably they aspire to live that kind of life and yet they have no idea what is required of a true Warrior-Lover.

Another example is even less flattering. President George W. Bush may or may not be a great man, but when he appeared in full flight gear from the seat of a fighter plane newly landed aboard a US aircraft carrier, where the sign 'Mission Accomplished' hung prominently – well, that has long been seen as an act of hubris that was the most obvious kind of public relations move. Several years later the Iraq war is still in progress and many people wonder what if anything has been 'accomplished.' Bush's action allowed him to appear as the worst kind of glory seeker. He and his party have had a difficult time living that one down. The true Warrior-Lover does not swagger around like a bully in a playground.

Returning to another pseudo-Warrior we'll recall that Oedipus, after killing his father next solves the Sphinx's riddle and, feeling good about himself, marries the widowed Jocasta – actually his mother. While this may be a match based on attraction it is certainly not a healthy attraction! Jocasta could be seen as one of those high-status women who get to claim high-status men as their mates. But as far as her inner qualities go, there's not much evidence that Jocasta has ever done anything at all apart from marrying one king and then marrying another.

The hint is clear – if one aspires to be a Warrior-Lover then one has to choose a life-partner who is an equal in personal development, not just in status. Everyone expected Oedipus to marry Jocasta, and so he did. I am reminded of all those good, wealthy families, with excellent connections, who married their sons and daughters off in exactly the same way, sometimes with less than happy results. Jocasta is a trophy wife. We'll recall that when the truth comes out about who Oedipus really is, she kills herself. It's a strong suggestion that she hasn't the inner resources to deal with public disgrace and perhaps find wisdom through hard work; she'd rather die. In contrast to this Oedipus blinds himself – which is symbolic of his need to look inwards – and so his search for inner meaning (the Pilgrim's task) can really begin.

The transition from Pilgrim to Warrior-Lover is perilous, and the example of Oedipus tells us exactly how we can fool ourselves that we have made it when we have done no such thing. The example of Antigone lets us know that we have to be prepared for defeat if we choose this path, and that there are some things more important than preserving one's own skin. For most of us this will probably not mean that we actually risk our lives, although we may have to risk our careers if what we believe in collides with what the world outside seems intent on doing. Brave reporters and news writers have routinely run into this in their struggles to present the truth; an illustration of this is the fight between Senator Joseph McCarthy and TV anchor Ed Murrow.

The necessity of balancing the Warrior and the Lover aspects is poignantly depicted in Botticelli's magnificent canvas *Venus and Mars*, painted about 1485. In the painting Mars lies back fast asleep, perhaps exhausted after a hard day's fighting, armor scattered around him, or perhaps he has passed out after lovemaking. Venus sits looking bored, clearly disappointed that the virile god of war is not more attentive to her. We can see Mars as the cliché of the male who has sex and then goes straight to sleep, ignoring the woman once he's got what he wants. Of course, there's no guarantee that they have had sex. Venus is wearing rather too many clothes, and doesn't look at all as if she's just had a wild and satisfying romp. By contrast Mars is wearing very little. Whatever we decide about what they have or have not just done with each other we can certainly say that they are not in loving accord in the picture. It could be that this painting was simply an excuse to paint a very beautiful woman and man, but there may be more it has to convey to us. It doesn't take a huge leap of the imagination to see in it the bored wives of Italy feeling neglected by their powerful but politically-obsessed husbands at that time, in the same way that trophy wives today are less real partners than adjuncts to a game rooted in display and gain. And we can also see the picture as the failure of men and women to understand each other and work together. This remarkable canvas gives us a memorable image of the unbalanced Warrior who fails to make real contact with the Lover. When the Lover aspect is not attached to the purposeful drive of the Warrior, the Lover becomes merely a sensualist and the Warrior slips into the role of the restless fighter. Each half of the archetype needs the other.

If we choose to let the painting work on us it is as strong a plea as any I have come across for the necessity of these two opposites to join together. At the time Botticelli was painting, Italy was riven by armed conflicts of all kinds that turned communities into battlegrounds. It was also a society that loved luxury and sensual indulgence. And so there were those who fought viciously just in order to indulge themselves, the two aspects of the archetype remaining estranged from each other. It's a poignant painting, full of the sadness of failed connection, allegorical of the ills of his society, and of ours too.

A similar story is related in a different way in George Eliot's novel *Daniel Deronda* (1876) when Gwendolyn Harleth's marriage to a wealthy aristocrat seems to be exactly the fairy-tale marriage – yet it is clear the two have no love for each other. Instead it is Daniel's union with the penniless Mirah that shows two people joined in religious belief and moral purpose as well as in mutual attraction. Eliot visits the same territory in *Middlemarch* when Dorothea Brooke marries the promising scholar and cleric Casaubon, only to discover that he wants her as his assistant in his scholarship, and does not love her at all. Yet all the townspeople think it a brilliant match. When Casaubon dies and Dorothea finds she loves Will Ladislaw, she decides to marry him despite the loss of the enormous inheritance, which Casaubon tied into her remaining single. They marry for love, and also because that love is based in their awareness of their sense of a social obligation to better the conditions of those who are less fortunate than they are. In loving each other Will and Dorothea are finally able to support each other's visions for a better world and extend their loving natures productively, usefully, to benefit the wider community. They become peaceful fighters for progress. Love and a larger social commitment are the hall-marks of the Warrior-Lover.

George Eliot reinforces the point by having another pair of lovers in the story: Doctor Lydgate and Rosamond Vincy. He is brilliant and wants to do good deeds; she is beautiful and socially ambitious. They marry and the Lover archetype is for a while strong in them. As time goes by, however, we discover that Lydgate spends more and more time working with rich patients to ensure that his wife has the comforts she needs, and less and less time working on advancing medicine, which is what he truly cares about. Lydgate calls his wife his little basil plant, after the Keats poem *Isabella*. As Eliot's readers at that time would have known, Isabella places the severed head of her murdered lover, whom she was not permitted to marry, in a pot, and she plants basil on top. Lydgate, when asked why he calls his wife a basil plant, replies that basil feeds on dead men's brains. It's a shocking response. He sees how his wife has destroyed his ambitions, yet he doesn't seem able to change that in any way, since he sees himself as already dead. This is a poignant example of the Warrior-Lover failing to achieve balance or understanding because the sexual Lover has been allowed to overwhelm the Warrior. Lydgate has descended to the level of the spouse who blames his wife for everything – and that puts him firmly in the Orphan stage. Sexual fascination can leave the archetype unbalanced, and so the quality we need to be aware of here is the Warrior's need to define personal limits. The Warrior-Lover may require balance but it's an archetype that demands the Warrior's fierceness if that balance is to be properly maintained. That's what we see in Antigone. She simply will not give in on certain important points.

If we are to understand how the Warrior-Lover operates we can do so by considering the images we have of fighting men and women, and using those images as metaphors that reflect a spiritual reality. We can do the same with the image of the Lover.

In our culture the soldier is seen as disciplined, trained, highly practical, conversant with all sorts of hardware of a ferocious sort, and she or he is supposed to be an unflinching individual. In almost every story or movie about the military there is a point at which the Warrior has to take stock of what weaponry he has and decide how to use it. This usually occurs just before the climactic face-off with the enemy. The secret weapon is prepared, the sword is sharpened and the warhorse is given an extra helping of oats. In the medieval romances of knights and maidens this is called "arming the knight" and it's often described in loving detail. It's a convention that survives today in Hollywood. For instance, in *Saving Private Ryan* the small troop of American GIs survey their combined weaponry and decide how they are going to use their resources and skills best. As a scene that reminds the audience how dangerous their situation is, it works well. But there is more here to ponder. Let's take this example as a metaphor for what we all must do, if we are to be Warriors: we'll have to look inside ourselves, decide what our best and strongest personal resources are and *how to commit them*. This is crucial, for struggles in life are not won simply because one side has all the weaponry and money. They are won or lost because of the way the combatants use what they have. Think about the US presence in Iraq and you'll see what I mean. Superior technology and firepower are never enough on their own.

Just as a soldier coolly cleans, adjusts, and assesses his weapons, so the Warrior must be detached enough to be able to see his mental strengths and decide how to use them.

The Lover aspect is there to temper the Warrior. After all, in life's struggles we don't just want to crush the opposition; ideally we'd like to win them over then we don't *have* to fight every last one of them! One has only to think of the White House's phrase that the Iraq invasion was to win the 'hearts and minds' of the Iraqis. Winning the heart is distinctly the language of courtship, of love. In this case we can see that the Lover aspect is empathic, idealistic, compassionate, and wants to *be* loved in return.

Traditionally these two roles of Warrior and Lover have been split for ease of reference. The knight fights the dragon first and then gets to marry the maiden he's rescued, which is a little too simplistic. Perhaps Shakespeare's comedies can help us here because the men – who have often just been in armed and violent struggles – have to be educated and tamed by the women they love. In Shakespeare's view the men have to be tamed and the women have to be heard before harmony can reign. The twin aspects of male and female have to acknowledge each other and fuse. Orlando in *As You Like It* has to listen to the disguised Rosalind in order to find out who Rosalind is as a person. If she'd not been disguised he'd have responded to her only as a love-object to be wooed.

Also, in the legends of the Knights of the Round Table, the quest of Sir Galahad for the Holy Grail involves him rescuing maidens and even marrying one, except in his case he does not consummate the marriage until after he has found the Grail. Some have seen this as a standard Christian rejection of sex and sexual love, and certainly that is a possible interpretation. Yet we can see it a little differently, perhaps as a metaphor indicating that Sir Galahad's role as a Lover has to develop *simultaneously* with his Warrior's quest for purity. It cannot be just one or the other. In struggling to locate the Grail, Sir Galahad is growing his capacity for devotion. When he has found the Grail and learned its secret, then he will be fit to experience real earthly love in a new way. He fights for the Grail and for his wife. It's a reminder that finding sexual love can sometimes cause many of us to give up, temporarily, the search for our personal truth. The wisest thing we can do is to recognize that both aspects of the self have to develop together, and that they can – they must – fuel each other.

In the ordinary world we can see this sometimes with those couples who take the time to talk with each other, perhaps each day at dinner, about what they've each been doing in the work that is closest to their hearts. They may find that talking with their partner generates more insights, more wisdom. I have witnessed writers and artists sharing this sort of communication, and doctors, and therapists too. At times it seems more as if one is observing a business meeting than a conversation, since the partners work together effectively as a team. Loving what they do, they bring that love to the person they love, and they allow it to grow.

So, how does one find that other person and how does one fight for the person one loves?

The first step is perhaps the most basic: one identifies a person who is worthy of one's love rather than merely responding to attraction or sexual availability. The Warrior-Lover makes conscious choices about who he or she is going to love, and such decisions are not based on mere convenience. They depend upon assessments, and on soul-recognition. If we know we're looking for someone who is our equal or even our superior then we need to consider in some detail who that person is likely to be before we go looking, so that we will recognize the qualities we want when they appear. Just as important is that we must be aware of how we expect to feel when we are in the presence of someone who will bring us forward, someone who will spur us to be more than we might otherwise be, so that when we find ourselves surprised we don't immediately run away. Soldiers feel nervous before combat, as do athletes before a match. Knowing this, they prepare for it so they don't panic when the moment arrives.

Where many of us go wrong is in recognizing and being attracted to those people who are actually weaker than we are because we think we can dominate the relationship. John Bradshaw puts it this way: every time you look around a room and find yourself feeling attracted to someone, the chances are you are responding to that person's weakness. That person may well be sending out signals that say, "I don't expect that much. I'm a nice person. I'm not fierce in any way." Genetically that may have been a message that helped humans reproduce; who knows for sure? Certainly it's a recipe for a nice cozy non-threatening romance. But what about those people we meet whom we find ourselves feeling challenged by? I don't mean that they behave outrageously or throw things around – that's another kind of challenge. What I'm referring to is those people who, when we interact with them, require that we be fully present, thinking, and truly ourselves. Often we reduce this to the pat formula of "opposites attract" because it's hard not to be fully alert when faced with someone who is very different from ourselves. It goes deeper than this, however. We can easily choose to love and struggle for those who fit neatly into our life and world view, and we'll be acting like Orphans if we do so. Yet what about the riskiness of choosing to commit to loving someone who won't let us stay in our comfortable mindset, who won't let us get away with short-changing ourselves?

Rudyard Kipling's poem *Mandalay* (1898) is a humorous reminder of this. In it a semi-literate Cockney soldier reminisces about the romance of the East, and of Burma in particular. What we see is that the *place* has worked its magic on him and, back in England, he can't fit in anymore. He's fallen in love with the East and his "neater, sweeter maiden in a cleaner, greener land." The experience has challenged everything he thought he knew, and as he listens to the housemaids chattering about their boyfriends he all but snarls:

> Tho' I walks with fifty 'ousemaids outer Chelsea to the Strand,
> An' they talks a lot o' lovin', but wot do they understand?
> Beefy face and grubby 'and –
> Law'! Wot do they understand?

Love is not just an invitation to take on a fixed rate mortgage and a shared retirement scheme. It's a drill sergeant's order to go out and work hard at something that has no sure-fire guarantee of success, but which will test each of us to our limits.

Kipling's soldier regrets leaving Mandalay and his lover, feels himself isolated in London, and ponders the remote possibilities of return. Could he go back, now? If he'd never left he'd surely have been pursued and perhaps shot as a deserter. If he went back (if he could afford to) he'd be considered as having "gone native." In fact he hasn't the courage to follow his heart's desire; he's caught between his wishes and his sense of himself as an Englishman. But for a moment he experienced something that stirred his Cockney soul into poetry:

> If you've 'eard the East a-callin' you won't never 'eed ought else…
> On the road to Mandalay,
> Where the flyin' fishes play
> And the dawn comes up like thunder, outer China 'crost the bay!

How easy it is to lose love when we hold conventional views, Kipling seems to say. The Cockney has been a soldier – a Warrior – and he's been a Lover, but he's missed the opportunity to remain in that space. Is it the East that calls to him, or is it the memory of who he was becoming before he turned back? If all this makes love sound rather frightening I'd simply say that, yes, it is meant to be so at this point; it's only easy if you're choosing the Orphan sort of love. And, with all respect, that may be what many people need. Sometimes those who have joined together as Orphans, trying to avoid too much upset in their lives, find that together their courage can grow. Together they can explore who they are as individuals and as a couple; growth can happen in many ways. When the growth starts, however, it can be hard to deal with.

Here's an example of what I mean by that. A woman in one of my writing classes long ago came to see me to ask if her husband could attend classes with her. While this wasn't actually school policy, I didn't think it would hurt anyone, so I asked her why he wanted to attend. Her reply shocked me. She said, "He sees that going to college is changing me, and he wants to know what's going on." So the husband came to class, sat quietly, and looked worried. Three weeks later, the woman was back in my office. "I have to drop out of your course, and out of college," she said. At first, she wouldn't say why, but eventually she admitted that her husband was truly uncomfortable with the person she'd become – questioning, more empowered – and he blamed the college. Her final words to me were that she had to quit school to save her marriage.

This is an unusual example but one that has haunted me ever since. A marriage that was based on one partner being a bit of a ditz, and the other being the solid provider who liked that role – well, that sounds a bit like an Orphan marriage to me, and one that *could not* grow without altering its existing form – so it didn't. An emerging Pilgrim was not able to take the risk of losing what she had.

Being comfortable means that there is no real change; being uncomfortable may mean you're in a new place, thinking, assessing and learning. Discomfort for its own sake is not what I'm advocating. I'm suggesting that one can become acclimatized to change and growth. Growth need not be violent or frenetic, yet it will happen if we don't seek to shut it down – and even if we do it has a way of growing anyway, like grass between paving slabs. The Warrior-Lover's path therefore is one of constant vigilance, constant growth, and of delight in that growth. There are always new things to be learned. And why shouldn't a couple be delighted to spend several decades together working out life's many fascinating aspects, developing their personal levels of awareness and intimacy?

Yet examples are rare.

We can all think of examples of the opposite: couples who have raised their children, done an excellent job at it, and who then decide that their relationship has run its course. So they divorce. These people may have been true Warrior-Lovers in the task of raising their children. They may be acting as truly courageous people in refusing to accept a marriage that they feel has worn itself out, but they haven't managed to become Warrior-Lovers in their own relationship. They may need to go on another pilgrimage to become Warrior-Lovers in their next relationship, or they may choose a comfortable Orphan relationship. A woman I worked with who had just finished a messy divorce put it like this: "I just want a relationship now that's settled and comfortable. I want things to be easy." And so she did settle, happily, for a man twenty years her senior who was steady, a good stepfather to her children, and whom she described as "very easy to get along with." A safe harbor for a storm-tossed vessel, one could say.

So here we must state the obvious. The Warrior-Lover can't become fully him or herself alone. It requires a vital relationship with another, although it does not have to be a sexual relationship. Men can mentor other men, women can do the same, and any variation on the theme that works is just fine. But they don't all work. A Warrior-Lover linked to an Orphan finds insufficient challenge for the relationship to be truly satisfying and so becomes restless, resentful and sometimes destructive; the Warrior rampages and the Lover wilts. True Warrior-Lovers seem to work in pairs; they are devoted to truth now and into the future also.

Perhaps the aspect that most confuses us is that these patterns of spiritual growth do not seem to be illustrated in a straightforward way in our culture. They exist in our literature and in our folk-tales, but why are they not made more obvious in the rest of life? There is the ghost of a tradition still observable that allows for the individual to move from one version of the self to another, from Orphan to Pilgrim to Warrior-Lover. The Catholic Church, with its first Communion ceremony makes a gesture towards what was once, clearly, a rite of passage, in which the individual is, after a period of religious training and introspection, adopted as a full member of the religious community. The new communicant is expected now to champion the beliefs of the Church, but not, alas, to question them. The Bar Mitzvah works the same way.

Now let us consider the vestigial reminder of changed status that exists in the ritual of the stag party. In the eighteenth century this was still revered as a traditional dinner given by the groom-to-be to say farewell to those friends he would no longer be able to spend time with when he was married. It was, therefore, a last hurrah for the rowdy band of brothers and a welcoming of a new attachment that rendered the old ties obsolete. It was a trading up from one kind of companionship or adoption to another form of attachment, as valued as the symbolic "giving away of the bride" at a wedding. The best man's speech at weddings these days is an excuse for laughter and fun, and yet its origin lies in the desire of those friends from the groom's former life to bestow their blessing on the union – an affirmation that they accept the change in his situation. One may say this is slim evidence, yet I'd point out that almost everyone gets married so it has a universal applicability. And when one leaves one's youthful companions in this way it is usually because one is planning the start of one's own family. By definition one is no longer someone else's child, but is now planning to be someone's parent, with all the demands that involves.

The point is simple: the letting go of old associations, like the letting go of old wounds, demands a change of attitude. It's a growth point, even if it seems to be treated these days as an excuse to get outrageously drunk. The marriage ceremony is a huge celebration, and yet it is also the point at which both partners are agreeing to take on the most demanding responsibilities most of us will ever face, socially, personally, and financially. Divorce is a comparatively recent phenomenon, which has tended to make us forget the extent of the ties that are brought into action by marriage. We may think that a wedding is all about love, and we'd be right. Yet behind that vision we can see (if we choose to look) that it is also a public acknowledgement of personal growth into responsibility. If we choose to see this as a symbolic move, then it would be hard not to see it as a series of steps. Each person has been an Orphan; each has gone on a pilgrimage searching for a mate; and each has thought about who she might be while on that search. When this Pilgrim agrees to take responsibility for her life and to link with a mate for the rest of their lives together, then she moves into the Warrior-Lover state of being committed to the marriage and the person.

Notice that a marriage ceremony is about the *future* of those concerned. It does not ask, "Do you love this person?" It asks if the participants are prepared to take on a commitment for the future. Many people these days choose to write their own marriage vows. I take this to be a healthy sign since they are saying, in effect, *this* is what I'm contracting to do, and here's my promise that I will. The Warrior, by definition, has to pledge some sort of allegiance to a cause; the Lover takes that pledge into the realm of personal commitment.

The Warrior-Lover therefore has several aspects and it's most convenient to discuss these in terms of them as a pair. As a spouse, this person will venture all she has for her lover. There are no half measures, here. This person will fight for her spouse and fight alongside her spouse for those things they both love – especially children. Yet just as no soldier can function alone, so this couple relies on mutual support. They "have each other's back" and any desertion from this arrangement is met with disbelief, anger and grief. But we should be aware that the Warrior and Lover aspects can settle out – one person in the couple becomes the bread winner, the aggressive go-getter, and the other raises the children virtually alone. This isn't satisfactory because it pushes each person into a role, and a role is usually static, limited, ultimately the realm of the Orphan. A true Warrior-Lover is always eager for growth; stasis is not really an option. Warrior-Lovers, working together, allow each other space and really can work as buddies as well as Lovers. They ask, expecting to receive; they give, knowing that they can also take in equal measure. Above all, they know they have to help each other keep the balance of Warrior and Lover within, and they will be committed to this as they grow. They don't put up with stasis just as in the everyday world soldiers can't bear being stuck around a barracks block and lovers can't put up with the same old activities all the time. This is the archetype that sees living as 'a vale of soul-making' as John Keats put it, a place we have to venture out into so that we can grow our souls fully.

How can we illustrate this best? Consider the good teacher. Here is a person who will give a huge amount of support and real love. Good teachers actually enjoy the subjects they teach and they enjoy being with their students as learners. Yet the truly excellent teacher does not force the information on others. She, instead, seeks to interest and encourage others so they can enjoy the information and learn through engaging with it. Obviously, there's a power imbalance – the teacher is older and knows more and has a curriculum to complete – yet the excellent teacher works in a loving way and has enough distance from the students to allow them their own lives and thoughts *outside* school. And truly excellent teachers will often report how much they learn from their students – it's never just a one-way street where one person has all the answers. Now, imagine two really good teachers, teaching each other by the free and unconstrained exchange of ideas, thoughts and feelings, questioning, respecting and allowing the other space. That's the Warrior-Lover in action.

"Teaching" of course, puts an unfair spin on the process. Remember – the Warrior must be resolute and work with controlled emotions, whereas the Lover can be playful and value effusive emotion more than rationality or logic. The challenge is to know when to use each aspect appropriately. This is the perfect mesh of body and soul, fantasy and pragmatism, logic and emotion. Carl Jung suggested that this is the essential life-work for all human beings – to be able to integrate these seemingly opposite aspects of ourselves, so that we can live as whole beings. When the teacher learns, when the Lover can be determined without being overbearing, when the Warrior can be compassionate without being foolish, then we have the necessary balance.

Obviously this is not something that can be learned in a weekend workshop. Men are from Mars (Warriors) and women are from Venus (Lovers) right? Well, no. Unbalanced development and the polarization of roles leads to that sort of artificial separation and it is our life task to get back to something more integrated than this. The popularity of John Gray's workshops and books is ample proof that in our society we have lost sight of what the balanced Warrior-Lover archetype really is, and we are desperate to rediscover it with all its vital energy.

Consider the archetype this way: the wise military leader is likely to be the one who spends a fair amount of time trying to work out what the opposition is going to do next – and to that end will gather intelligence, send out spies, and seek to penetrate the other's mind. This version of the Warrior has to understand the opponent *and* himself, as well as his own goals. Now, if we translate that image back into something more peaceful, such as a relationship between those who care about each other, then we have a truly potent comparison. Imagine, if you can, a loving relationship in which both people are truly listening to each other – both to what is said and what is left unsaid. Imagine a relationship where each partner knows just how dangerous it can be to hold preconceptions about who the other is. Think about the huge amount of awareness this would entail. It would involve each person being fully present to what is happening in that moment, as well as being alert to what has happened in the past and the possible ways this could play out in the future. Isn't it sad that we know how to do this but we routinely reserve this vast amount of attention only for those we have designated as our enemies, or as the opposition, or as terrorists? Our society is extremely effective at living out the unbalanced Warrior role, which because it is only a role becomes, inevitably, just another aspect of the Orphan. Of course we should watch out for those who wish to destroy us; and we also have to use the same care to nurture our relationships with those we love.

Unfortunately we also routinely aim very low in our expectations of what a couple can be. The "Happy Marriage" in our society is generally depicted as something very undemanding. The contented pair, communicating in the sort of shorthand that has developed over years, is seen puttering towards their golden wedding in a spirit of live and let live. This is admirable; the trouble is that unless we are aware of the hard work that goes into achieving this we may miss the important point. One can only get to the full expression of the Warrior-Lover after having gone through the struggles, the misunderstandings, the frustrations, the moments of unbelievable joy and of shattering grief that have allowed this couple to be fully themselves in each other's presence.

If we can hold in our minds the image, the metaphor, of the Warrior-Lover, it can be extraordinarily helpful in showing us how to get to that point.

Bear in mind, as well, that the image can also warn us about how misuse of this stage can separate loving couples, even when they may elect to stay together. Consider the Regimental reunion, or the Veterans' Day get-togethers that have all the old soldiers at one table and their wives at another. This physical displacement can sometimes be seen as a mirror of the lack of communication between couples on certain points. How can the old soldier – probably suffering from some form of post-traumatic stress disorder, since almost all soldiers who have faced combat are changed by it to some degree – how can he communicate his emotions about such events to his spouse? Anecdotal observations suggest that it is extraordinarily difficult. If the old soldier can be open about his psychic wounds to those who are truly trying to be close to him, he has a chance of being able to fuse the Warrior and the Lover fully.

So why do old soldiers not speak up about what they know, and what can we learn from them? I'd suggest that the Warrior's experience is of the dark side of himself. He experiences the fear of violent death, pain, and dismemberment. He confronts the possibility that his death may not matter in the slightest, that his cause is wrong and his life decisions suicidal. He faces the possibility that there is no God, no goodness, no purpose in the world, and that cruelty and death are stronger by far than love and life. He peeps into hell. Then he has to live with that knowledge of himself as one who has felt fear and who also wanted to be a killer. Perhaps he actually was a killer, and has to live with that. No wonder those fresh-faced lads of "The Greatest Generation" came back looking so haunted. In the 1949 classic 'Twelve O'Clock High' about the US bomber crews of World War II, Gregory Peck's portrayal of a group leader is a chilling version of this. In a memorable scene he addresses his crews by saying that they'll find their task of flying bombing missions much easier if they consider themselves 'already dead.' The Warrior has to know death, close up. How can one possibly return to the daily world from such a difficult place? Robert Bly claims that Celtic and Viking warriors of old went through complicated 'cooling down' rituals, supported by their families, so that they could integrate their experiences in battle with the ordinary world; unfortunately Bly gives no references. With the toll of traumatized veterans from Iraq rising every day, we could use that information. All we can claim is that today there seems to be no mechanism or template for returning to the everyday world.

Traumatic experience is certainly available for women, since war is cruel to civilians too. Moreover women face childbirth, which until comparatively recently was often very dangerous – and certainly painful. Yet with childbirth there is a reward in the form of a child, and that changes the comparison. The passage towards possible death is rewarded with love and life.

In fact, this experience of helplessness is the Warrior-Lover's most important test. Each person, male or female, who takes this route, will have to endure a season in hell. In one image it is the experience of the soldier facing death, "The Great Death" as Stephen Crane calls it in *The Red Badge of Courage*. Answering him across time is Sonia Sanchez's aging black woman in *Just Don't Never Give Up on Love,* who describes a similar period of shattering despair in her life as 'the slaughterhouse.' I think the title of Sanchez's piece spells out at least one of the themes we're considering here: anyone can face death in any number of ways; the important thing is to take away the lesson that it is, in the end, just death, the exact negation of everything we've been taught to value.

Our most common experience of this is probably when we see a loved one die. It's not an experience one forgets and it takes some effort to deal with the information. When a parent dies we all are faced with something that may be intellectually accessible – that the older person must die and leave us – and yet it is often emotionally hard to understand the change this will bring. For instance, I knew my father was going to die; he'd been sick for some time. Yet when it happened I felt unexpectedly naked. He'd been a big presence in my life, and now he was gone. The things that were incomplete in our relationship would now have to be dealt with just by me, with no one to blame, no excuses, no prevarications.

His approach to death also caused me to have to face some troublesome questions. As he became less well, as his memory faded, as his vitality diminished to a shadow of what it had been I was forced to ask myself the same sorts of questions he was surely asking: without my body, memory, possessions, achievements, who am I? What came out of this is the awareness that, as we die, if we're fortunate, we are reduced to a more essential part of ourselves, and that self is one that wants to be loved and to give love. We all want someone to hold our hand and soothe our brow as we get closer to death, and nothing matters much except those we have loved. All the old quarrels one might have had, all the resentments, they all slip away. Only the need to love remains. Perhaps this is why so many anecdotes exist of dying people seeing their family members waiting for them at the bed-side, or talking with long lost friends. Whether you choose to believe that these are returning spirits, or that these are illusions created by the dying person, is probably much less important than that we see it as confirmation of the need, at the end of life, to feel love.

Experiencing the death of a child or a friend can be shattering also, and perhaps far more disorienting than the death of a parent. We may find ourselves doubting the Universe as a good place. We face our loneliness, our insignificance. We see a world that seems to be in chaos, we're scared, and we are tempted into the darkest despair. What if there's only pain and sorrow in this world? The Warrior knows she has to carry on anyhow, and the best response is to turn to the Lover aspect of the self. Life is pointless without Love, so we have to put our trust in Love. Love is seemingly weak, but we know it outlasts death. It outlasts everything. Love really is everything, and *that* calms the fires of hell. Knowing that Love is all there is makes it doubly sweet. Love cures the Warrior's wounds.

The Challenges for the Warrior-Lover:
The Special Relationship

The Warrior-Lover is a stage that has its own pitfalls to face in some unexpected ways. It's quite possible for a couple to each achieve the balance of Warrior-Lover in themselves and then to become stuck in that sense of specialness that can come along with knowing one has an exceptional partnership. Any entwined relationship may seem at first sight to be extraordinary but, alas, it may leave no room for anyone else in it. Partners can become so dependent upon each other that they then find themselves rejecting other possible interactions since these seem inferior to what they already have. Of course, they'd be right to think like that. The union of two Warrior-Lovers is pretty impressive. But that doesn't mean that the non-sexual relationships the pair can have are not worth considering. Ironically, it is the valuing of what they have with each other that may blind them to what else is available. This is a potentially dangerous form of isolationism as within it there can be the tendency for the couple to feel pride at how well they think they are relating, and as they feel superior there is perhaps a temptation to be judgmental of others. Left unchecked they may blind themselves to the ego-gratification they derive from viewing their relationship this way. They congratulate themselves on being so special, so much more advanced than what they think others are capable of achieving. Well, this can rapidly turn out to be another version of the Orphan's view, in which the couple values the relationship for what it demonstrates to others rather than for what it can do as a living entity. Sometimes I have come across couples who are fiercely proud of their relationship, and who look at first glance to be Warrior-Lovers. Yet closer examination will reveal that the relationship is not, in fact, producing any meaningful effect beyond their front door. The true Warrior-Lover, after all, does not fight just for the medals. The Warrior-Lover is supposed to be striving for a worthy cause that is bigger than the personal reward, one that makes the world a better place, a more humane place. If one loses sight of this the result is likely to be a sort of cozy conspiracy that can quickly slip into self-congratulation – and that's the Orphan's way of doing things.

When any of us has a special relationship like this we are likely to feel that we are important because we matter to the other person: this pleases our ego. Our partner makes us feel good about those parts of ourselves we may not feel particularly good about, otherwise why would we need a partner to reassure us? And in that way we begin to see our specialness as important in itself, and we contrast it to other people who are less 'special' than we are, in our judgment. Remember: when we judge like that we are not using compassion, and compassion is an essential component of the balanced Warrior-Lover's life. What most of us don't do in a situation like this is to take the information we are getting and use it appropriately. So our partner makes us feel good about those aspects of ourselves we don't feel good about? That's information worth knowing. The task now is, how I can feel good about the whole of me without needing someone else to give me consoling flattery? If I can love myself, faults and all, that will help me to love not only my partner but also other people who need love, help, and encouragement. If I am at peace with myself I can be more present to any other person I meet, not just my partner. Being a Warrior-Lover is not a closet activity, although it may be fostered first in the private realm of love. It is an activity that demands growth just as human beings need exercise; otherwise they will atrophy.

Special relationships have a sad way of falling to pieces. Since the ego desires the sense of being thought unique, what tends to happen is that two people who crave this reassurance get together and enter into a sort of dishonest pact. They seem to think this way: if I agree to be nice about your frailties and flatter you, then you have to do the same for me. The trouble is that each person knows that if the other person is so insecure and needy then ultimately that means the relationship is not as impressive as either would like to believe, and this causes resentment. In fact couples linked this way grow to hate the need they have for each other at the very same time as they profess to love the other and be above this kind of reassurance. Keeping the relationship stable then demands more and more time and effort, and it becomes exclusive to the extent that there is no real room for anyone else to matter or be noticed – neither children, nor friends, nor parents.

Even special relationships between Warrior-Lovers are at risk of slipping into Orphan patterns.

Points to Ponder:
Keeping the Balance

The situation of the Warrior-Lover is extraordinarily demanding, since during its maturation it involves almost a complete change from initial enthusiasm to quiet acceptance. The Warrior-Lover achieves that first exuberance when a Pilgrim decides to declare herself fully, and state what she is prepared to live or die for. This is a moment that can be filled with pride, with courage; and it can be a moment when one feels immense trepidation. The bride or bridegroom is likely to be elated at the wedding, determined to be the best spouse possible, but that hopeful person does not yet know to what extent this new life will test his or her character.

In living this new life the Warrior-Lover will discover unexpected depths of feeling. The new spouse will find – to her surprise – reserves of energy that he or she never dreamed of before as she nurses sick children, consoles an exhausted partner, and still keeps a job. The Warrior-Lover, therefore, will experience the full power of her own personal love for another person, at the same time as she will realize the important truth that it's not just one person who is receiving the love, now, it is the whole family. Dad and Mom don't go out and work hard just for little Jimmy. They do it for all the kids and for their spouse, and if that involves putting oneself second, or last, on many occasions, then that's what they do. In each case the loyalty starts as a personal attachment – the spouse to the other spouse, the soldier to her buddies, the individual to a cause – and grows until it is a loving attachment to the family, or to a unit, or to the ideal. Then it grows one step further. The loving parent is not just attached to the nuclear family but to the whole concept of what is right and good for the society that most immediately surrounds them. The devoted soldier is attached to the purpose the army itself embodies. The idealist is attached to putting the ideals into action for the good of everyone concerned.

There is an extraordinary poem by Richard Lovelace (1618-1658) that in some measure spells this out. Written as a love poem, supposedly, it is titled, "To Lucasta: on Going to the Wars". Lucasta was an invented name, of course, as was the convention of the times, and the poem can be read as a love poem or it can be seen as something more. Here it is:

Tell me not, Sweet, I am unkind
That from the nunnery
Of thy chaste breast and quiet mind
To war and arms I fly.

True, a new mistress now I chase,
The first foe in the field
And with a stronger faith embrace
A sword, a horse, a shield.

Yet this inconstancy is such,
As you too shall adore
I could not love thee, dear, so much,
Loved I not honour more.

As a love offering to a lady the poem works well. Yet if we take it that Lucasta was a fiction we can see it as a portrait of what a man might write to his lover under circumstances in which he felt he had to leave her to fight in support of his king. In many ways the key lines are the last four, since he says that in loving a principle of right conduct so much that he leaves her he is, in fact, loving her *more*. The hint is clear: the man who has no sense of morality about the larger issues of life is not worth loving. In the poet's view the one love feeds the other; the ability to love sexually allows him to experience loyalty, and that loyalty has to give way to a cause greater than his own desire to be with her. This in turn allows him to value personal love still more highly. The two loves feed each other and neither love is complete without the other. This seems to be an accurate description of what the Warrior-Lover has to move through in the terms we've been using.

It's a theme Lovelace returns to in another poem, "To Althea, from Prison" which – once again – seems to be about love but is in fact about his loyalty to King Charles. It is best known for its often-quoted last verse, which starts:

Stone walls do not a prison make
Nor iron bars a cage

Considering that Lovelace was almost certainly in prison at the time, locked behind stone walls and iron bars, and that the man he supported, King Charles, was under arrest also, these are brave words indeed. This is a moving description of the Warrior-Lover facing defeat and recognizing that there are some things more important than winning. Some defeats have more real courage and integrity to them than some victories. Harold Bloom says that the purpose of art for readers is 'to confront greatness'. In these two poems we can have no doubt at all about the greatness of Lovelace's soul.

Seventeenth Century British poets were remarkable for choosing to write so that the surface meaning of a poem is only ever part of its total value, and we are not twisting the poem when we look at it in this fashion. Lovelace was writing about the Warrior-Lover archetype from first-hand experience and he gives us a wonderful evocation of what it feels like to live in that place.

So we could say that for the Warrior-Lover personal love, once established, must continue to grow beyond the specific and exclusive union to the significant other. This love will be tested to breaking point. It may in fact break. But it will remake itself, stronger for having been tested. And we learn that love can't stop death or defeat, but it can change the meaning of both so that they are no longer so powerful. Perhaps this is what Jung meant when he suggested that one of our life tasks was to make friends with death. That way, when the time comes, we can let go of life without regret, fear, or anger and let the natural process of dying take us over.

The Warrior-Lover stage is the most complex we have yet looked at. If we are able to absorb all its lessons we are ready to move on to the level of the Monarch, which is another paired image although this time of the King and the Queen, since the same twinned aspects of male and female are required to move to a still higher level.

In The Bedroom:
Remaining Open, Being Oneself

Sexually the union of two Warrior-Lovers can be extremely moving. Warrior-Lovers will not engage in sex with just anyone. That is not their nature. For the Warrior-Lover the person one takes to bed is the person one is committed to and loves as a whole person, since the other person's sexuality is felt to be an integral part of the whole that is that person. This could be seen as respect, as good manners, or some could even see it as prudishness. The Warrior-Lover doesn't have flings, but wishes to feel a true, trusting connection to the other and will take the time to build that connection. This is true not just in the early stages of a relationship, but for each occasion that they become sexually intimate.

Since each partner is alive to whom the other is, and to whom she herself is, and the event occurs in an atmosphere of love and trust, the sexual experience can be very different from what other levels encounter. For one thing, many lovers do not know how to approach their love-making in this spirit of real connection. In some couple and sex therapy classes, for example, the basic introductory exercises work on harmonizing the energies between the two people. It's a starting point for many yoga based therapies, too. This coming into alignment with one's partner can be done in many ways but one of the most effective starting places is in harmonizing the breathing so that each partner is literally in rhythm with the other. If we take that as a physical expression of a mental state we can say that each person needs to be attuned to who the other is and who she herself is, as a first step, and then each has willingly to accept this. Listening to the in-and-out movement of one's own breathing, being aware of one's partner's breath, mirrors the even give and take of sexual contact, the easeful unhurried to and fro of taking and receiving pleasure in a mutual way. This may sound basic but those breathing exercises are a metaphor as well as a physical action; for so many people are out of harmony with their significant others and not fully aware of how to change the situation that they wind up feeling trapped. In my counseling practice I have come across couples who are out of phase with each other and even with them-selves. They turn up in their bedroom preoccupied, sometimes over-tired, and often expecting their partner to be a certain way – even if that doesn't correspond to reality. When I listen to them describe their situations I sometimes hear them speak about their sex life in terms of it being a demand made upon them. They come out with comments like: 'He seems to expect …' or 'She wants sex when I don't,' or 'She asks me to do things I don't care to do,' and one of the saddest ones is, 'He doesn't make time….' In all these instances I listen carefully to determine if one or both partners are approaching lovemaking with preconceptions about who they should be, and who they think the other person thinks they should be. If we add to that the sense that many people think that love is 'supposed' to be a certain way (depending upon which books, movies, videos, and TV programs they've encountered), and that both may have yearnings that are highly unreal-istic as a result, we can see that it would be a huge relief for all concerned if they could feel free enough to let go of all these expectations. Working with a troubled couple at one point we discovered that the man was attracted to his girlfriend's almost tomboy-like character, but he still wanted her to be a *Playboy* centerfold when she came to bed. This set image of who he felt she should be was in contrast to who she actually was, and he found it very hard to get past this. For her part, the woman wanted him to be fit and toned again, because he'd recently put on a fair amount of weight. But most of all she wanted him to find her attractive, and because of his own pre-programmed images he was not able to do this. Conse-quently she didn't feel appreciated and was not able to see him as attractive any more. The interesting part was that initially in their relationship he had told her that she was very attractive to him, even though this wasn't quite true. He had hoped that when she came to love him more deeply that fact alone would make her more attractive in his eyes. This is just a simple example of the sort of extra baggage that gets dragged into the bedroom by many people. In this instance the man simply wasn't able to be himself or to be present to the actuality of the situation before him.

The true Warrior-Lover is one who takes the time and the effort to observe who the other person is at that moment, then looks to see who she herself is, and accepts this. In extending that acceptance (for real acceptance is love) in a non-judgmental way it becomes possible for each partner to explore feelings and desires. Physical imperfections mean nothing when one feels that one's partner sees the whole of who one is and perceives that wholeness with joy. Shyness and reserve evaporate. The need to 'perform' or 'be good in bed' are no longer part of the thought processes, since those attitudes involve some sort of quantitative assessment – and that as we know is what Orphans value. Orphans will sometimes calculate the number of times they have had sex, or the number of orgasms, and they may tend to do this while disregarding the nature of the spiritual connection that was, or was not, achieved.

After all, sharing one's sexuality with another is very different from 'having sex,' especially as sex is not a thing to be owned or possessed, so it cannot literally be 'had'. Experiencing an event is something that can only exist in that specific moment. When I read in my local newspaper about a trend amongst newlyweds who were video-taping their first sexual acts together as man and wife, I was interested that the emphasis for these people had shifted from what they were doing at the time, to the wish to create a physical artifact, one that presumably they could return to view when they felt the need. Far be it from me to judge anyone's sexual preferences – I'm merely pointing out that an emotional experience can in this process be turned into a physical object, in the same way that sharing one's self and one's sexuality is changed into 'having sex.' Orphans may need videotapes or DVDs to remind them, to reassure them; Warrior-Lovers know that the really important part of the lovemaking is not just the physical part. For the Warrior-Lover sexual consummation is felt as a point at which two people connect, and in that connection they transcend the ordinary. They know that something important has happened between them, and that each has been vulnerable and open – and accepted.

When this union occurs there is an interesting transformation, which is that the sense of safety and confidence that exists between the Warrior-Lovers allows for the long buried Innocent to emerge. I've heard people describe this as 'being like a kid again' and it marks the point at which that pure, loving Innocent is freed to venture forward once more. The Warrior-Lover is able to access the very considerable strength of that archetype, without its vulnerabilities and limitations. In fact the Warrior-Lover can use the positive qualities of the Orphan and the Pilgrim too. She will revere the sense of safety the Orphan values, and she will honor the honest inquiry the Pilgrim lives by, but she will not allow either aspect to take over who she is.

Claiming the Archetype's Energy

If we wish to experience and feel the energy of the Warrior-Lover in our own lives we may wish to recall those people we came into conflict with, whom we later were able to make peace with. Do you have anyone like that in your life? If so, keep a mental picture of that person handy to remind you of the power you have when fighting and the necessity for remaining open and loving. One man recounted how the person at his prep-school whom he most hated became the person he found he most trusted and loved, even though it took years to get to that point. Freshman college photos can sometimes fulfill the same role, as we survey who we finally became friends with, and why.

Again, you can choose to select a time when you had to persuade others to do things the way you thought was best, and even though you may have argued at times, you were able to maintain your stance and still were able to remain friendly. How did it feel to live that experience? Were you able to stay in a place of receptivity, to hear what others had to say? Remember, for the Warrior-Lover it is never simply a question of what the end product may be, but whether people were able to work together in a directed way. A different example of this is the man who had a photograph of a beautiful vintage car, which, he explained, he had bought using almost all his money. His friends had thought him mad to do so. He stuck to his hunch and several years later made a huge profit when it turned out to be a hot commodity that suddenly became fashionable. He was able to recall how he stuck to his own point of view, even when his friends were unsupportive, and how the money had allowed him to remake his life. In fact he had truly remade his own life when he had refused to do what he usually did in the past, which was to give in to peer pressure.

Another man recalled how he had to struggle to make a decent life for his wife and himself, since they were both writers and not making much money. He cherished the memories of that time, because they were doing what they felt they had to, living their lives the way they needed to, and even though they had not produced a best seller between them they had no regrets at all. That's the power of the Warrior-Lover. Whatever example you choose to think about, focus on it because of the energy it brought to your soul; and when you do that you reactivate the archetype and claim its power.

In my workshops I know just how difficult this can be. I have an exercise that I ask people to do, and it goes like this: participants are asked to pair with someone they don't know and then I give each person a few moments to think about something they did, or a particular time that made them feel good about what they had done. When each person has an event in mind I ask him or her to tell their partner about it for exactly two minutes. During this time the partner is not allowed to interrupt or take notes. After the first person has spoken, the second person then has two minutes to repeat back what she has heard. No interruptions, no commentary. The first person then gets to say whether the listener got things right or not. Then the roles are reversed. After we're all done I ask the participants to share anything they noticed during the exercise. I'm always interested to note how many people feel they can't be proud of anything, and how many others are afraid they'll be seen as boasting. I'm equally surprised at how generous so many people are in praising a partner for having spoken out.

If the exercise goes well – and usually it does – it allows each person to express something that he or she is proud of and to feel acknowledged by the listener. Often one hears about astonishing actions where bravery and intelligence have clearly been abundantly present, and these events have been tidied away into some corner of memory.

The exercise asks us to reassess our relationship to our sense of successful agency in the world we know, and is sometimes accompanied by smiles and tears as people remember how bold and incisive they truly were. They find themselves feeling good about what they did. They access their courage and their sense of having done something worthwhile – and that is almost always a compassionate action. In this way they learn to feel and to *claim* the energy of the Warrior-Lover archetype. It's a good exercise to return to from time to time, since courage, like so many things, tends to fade when we don't use it. A question to ask yourself is: do you routinely hold yourself to standards that include courage? If someone is acting in an offensive way, do you ask them, compassionately, if there might not be another way of doing things? Most of us don't.

The Warrior-Lover in the Tarot

Three cards, numbered six, seven and eight, all seem to reflect the path to the Warrior-Lover, and interestingly enough they split this archetype into complementary aspects. Card number eight is called Strength. On it we see a female figure, possibly a rendition of Nature, taming a lion. This is a representation of the strength and gentleness of the 'female' aspect of the self, taming and balancing the more 'male' energy of what is obviously a male lion.

The next card, The Chariot, number seven, shows a triumphant soldier driving a chariot drawn by two sphinxes, one white and one black. There is the bal-

THE LOVERS.

THE CHARIOT.

ance again, black and white, and it's clear that the soldier has control over the sphinxes and their potentially destructive nature, so he represents the civilizing force of moral strength. It is generally agreed that this is the card that reflects rational, logical and male attributes, and the absence of the emotional.

STRENGTH.

Card number six, The Lovers, shows two naked figures who are most probably Adam and Eve, with the tree of Knowledge in the Garden of Eden. This is confirmed because the tree comes complete with a serpent, behind the female figure, and another tree, possibly the Tree of Life, stands behind the male. Above them is an angel, who seems to be blessing them. There is no flaming sword of banishment here. What strikes us about the card is the balance, the symmetry. This is an image of lovers who are pure and equal and who have not yet lost their Eden; the angel blesses their straightforwardness.

Looking at these cards together we can see that Strength is an image of female power; the Chariot is certainly a male image; and Lovers in the Garden of Eden convey balance and purity. We recall that Adam and Eve were, for a while at least, faithful to each other and faithful servants to God; they were given dominion over all the animals on earth, also. They didn't need to exert themselves to control the other creatures because they were already in charge. The three cards seem to form a description of what the Warrior-Lover has to achieve, one step at a time. The female figure tames the lion, but does not kill it, representing the restraining of the emotions and also the necessity of a direct connection to the visceral emotional world. The soldier harnesses the power of mythical sphinxes, which were held to be evil spirits, and so the card could be seen as intellectual rigor in refusing dominance to merely destructive thoughts. The Lovers are shown as innocent, pure, and in close communion with God's will. The Lovers, of course, is the 'highest' card in the set of three, emphasizing the concept of these three as a progression.

The cards are immediate neighbors in the pack and each depicts a quality that can easily be turned into its opposite. They seem to say that strength is not the only way to control savagery, that triumph can become tyranny and arrogance, and that love can become self-indulgence (remember, Adam and Eve offended God because they assumed too much power). Balance between power and emotion is the recurrent theme. As such these three cards seem to reflect the Warrior-Lover's situation.

Experienced practitioners of the Tarot may find these readings to be somewhat different compared to what they are routinely used for. It's hard to say, since Tarot cards have meanings that depend upon where they appear in a reading's spread pattern, upon which pattern is used, and upon the deck one prefers – and that's before we take into account that each individual who consults the cards has a life situation that will cause the personal meanings of those cards to vary. The point here is not to challenge the wisdom of Tarot readers but to suggest that these cards may also hold another layer of meaning which functions in quite a different way. The task here has been to link the images on the cards to the archetypal stages we're looking at, and it's pretty clear that there is enough correspondence to give us meaningful, suggestive, and fruitful visual reminders of the archetype's essential qualities.

Examples from Real Life

Examples of the Warrior-Lover in real life are not always easy to spot. This is because the people who catch the public eye are often on their way through this stage, and dwell there for only a brief period of time before they become Monarchs. We can, however, still find several examples if we care to look. Angelina Jolie was certainly a very successful and troubled actress with her tattoos, her knife collection and her confused private life. At a certain point, though, she became more than just another Hollywood maverick and began taking an interest in adoption and in orphanages around the world. This seemed to coincide with her love affair with Brad Pitt, who is supportive but much less involved in charitable works. Would it be too much to say that an experience of success in love, which seems to have created lasting affection, has led her to be able to be more effective in the realm of public works and not just in movies? The widely-reported friction with Jon Voight, her father, may have made her feel like an Orphan in the past, and now it seems she is using her wound in a productive way. She has adopted three children as well as having one of her own. It's hard to know the exact motivations of public figures – their press agents always have a likely story to tell – so it remains to be seen whether Ms. Jolie will develop in the way she seems to be headed. Yet we can be sure that she is not just self-involved. Her critics in the press may try to say she is doing this just to be chic, but the sheer level of commitment required to raise four children, even when very wealthy, takes the discussion beyond a mere fashion statement. She has demonstrated the ability to grow a love that was personally based and bring it to the wider world, working as a UN Goodwill ambassador and championing the cause of refugees worldwide. Now other celebrities are also adopting children, and Madonna is one.

A more controversial example can be seen in the Clintons: when Bill Clinton had his affair with Monica Lewinsky, a number of archetypes bubbled to the surface in unexpected ways. Clinton committed a huge blunder in which, at a basic level, he did not truly see who Monica was or what she was likely to do. He was so filled with his own sense of himself as President – a Monarch situation if ever there was one – that he failed to see her as a human being who would be hurt and possibly vindictive. He thought he could get away with anything and when the ego arises in this way the Monarch archetype quickly becomes degraded.

Bill Clinton had proved himself to be an able politician and a man who wanted to serve his country. He was a Warrior-Lover at the very least, and as he rose in international stature he looked very much like a Monarch. Yet he deceived and disrespected at least one of the people he was responsible for protecting, at the same time as he was unfaithful to his wife for no real gain that anyone could point to. The result was far worse than anyone could have expected: while the Executive Branch was tied up in this scandal nothing was done about the massacres in the Balkans, for example.

Monica, we were told, had hopes that the President would leave his wife for her and that is about as extreme an example of Orphan thinking as one could imagine. The prince would come and whisk her away and all would be perfect.

Well, she was young and naïve and taken advantage of by the President and then by his foes, so she should not be blamed for the situation. The sad part was that Clinton did not see her as a person, or he'd have known she was a vulnerable Orphan and not even thought about spending any time with her. Clinton's ego blinded him to basic observation of those around him, and he lost sight of good judgment and real compassion. In different ways this could happen to anyone who is hero-worshipped. Whether it's a case of NBA stars who have sex with young women and then find themselves in court for paternity suits, or presidents having sex in the Oval Office, the situations are roughly the same, even if the results are worlds apart. People who are Monarchs in one area of their lives become targets for those Orphans who want to have their lives made easy.

Following all this Monica has not done very much with her celebrity. She launched a line of handbags, which had some success by trading on her name recognition, but she has faded from the public eye. Perhaps one day she will grow into a truly interesting figure; for now she's an Orphan, and shows few signs of being anything else.

Bill Clinton has emerged as a charming but diminished figure in many ways. We can see him as a Warrior-Lover who rose to be a Monarch for a while, before the scandal broke, and who then had to descend to Pilgrim level as he re-thought his life. Hillary, on the other hand, has shown signs of real growth. She has become a US Senator, of course, despite the carps and cavils of so many who would bring her down, and stepped forward to seek nomination as the Democratic Party presidential candidate. This engagement in meaningful work for her country showed her as a Warrior-Lover at the very least, and when Bill appeared at various locations to help with fundraising we saw that she could be loyal to her husband without being a push-over. The compassionate Lover had not subverted the Warrior within her. This demonstrated that she can use her own mind and not give in to her emotions in an undisciplined way. She has shown that she wants to serve her country and is not going to be deflected from that. Perhaps best of all for a politician, she has demonstrated that she can remain on a reasonable footing with her husband despite everything – which is a skill that serves her well and which she surely uses whenever she has to build consensus with others with whom she may personally disagree but whose overall policies she respects. It looks as if she has attained many of the attributes of the balanced Monarch.

Bill Clinton has had to redesign his life to some extent, and has decided to be a diplomat using his considerable skills to bring nations together in better understanding. In many ways he has rediscovered himself after spending time as a Pilgrim. He shows signs of rising again to be a Warrior-Lover and more. His renewed loyalty to Hillary and to meaningful work shows his compassion and his courage in the face of public criticism. We'll have to wait for history to pass the final verdict.

Perhaps the best place to see the Warrior-Lover in action is in memoirs written by people who have passed through that stage. Dennis Watlington, the Emmy winning TV and screen writer, records in his memoir *Chasing America* how he moved from black ghetto poverty, through astonishing hardships, and with the help of good luck, to success and a fulfilling life. Now he takes his life story to inner city schools and colleges, knowing full well that "whatever those kids have done, I've done it worse" and that he can show them the way forward. He describes himself as a Warrior for Peace, which is exactly who he is as he shows troubled disaffected kids that there is a better way forward. He describes in his memoir and in his talks how he was in prison back in the 60s when he first heard the Beatles singing "All You Need is Love." Up to that time he said he'd always thought that love was a stupid concept for dumb people, especially white people. "John Lennon showed me that you could be a man, and you could love. You didn't have to be mean to be a man. I couldn't believe I hadn't seen it like that before." Love, which he'd despised as the mark of weakness, had revealed itself to him as a strong force for healing; and he's held onto that ever since.

When Dennis speaks, and when he reads, you become aware that he is a survivor who has no intention of rubbing his past hardships in anyone's face. He's interested in where we can all go from here to make a productive future. He chooses not even to think about grinding axes or wallowing in past hurts, since he knows that leads to nothing that's good. It's remarkable to see how he has turned his personal hurts into public empowerment for those who lack it most obviously – be they black or white. As he says, "We've come a long way in a hundred years. Let's try to go further towards equality, and forget the past." Dennis has been a heroin addict and recovered twice, so he knows all about what it means to leave the past, purposefully, mindfully, behind.

In his work with the disadvantaged and with college students Dennis is a Warrior-Lover, and his effect on his audiences is that he encourages them to turn away from hopelessness and hurt. At those times he becomes a Magician, too, touching hearts in ways that surprise everyone.

Notes

1. *Oedipus Rex* and *Antigone* are both in *Sophocles, The Complete Greek Tragedies*, ed. David Grene and Richard Lattimore (Chicago: Chicago Univ. Press, 1991).
2. *Antigone* was most notably re-written by Jean Anouilh, who staged his version in Nazi-occupied Paris in February 1944 (not a timid act, given its theme of the

confrontation of tyranny), and there have been versions including one by Jean Cocteau and even an opera by Carl Orff.

3. *The Apprentice*, NBC TV January 2004, with Donald Trump.
4. Botticelli's *Venus and Mars* is in the National Gallery in London.
5. George Eliot, *Daniel Deronda* (1876), Penguin Classics edition, 1996.
6. George Eliot, *Middlemarch*, (1872), Signet Classics edition, 2003.
7. Interestingly, the subject of Sir Galahad and the Quest for the Holy Grail was painted as a series of decorations on the walls of the Boston Public Library in 1895, by Edwin Austin Abbey. Placed as it is the suggestion comes across that reading and scholarship are also quests for truth which demand purity of heart. It tells us that one can be a scholar Warrior-Lover.
8. John Bradshaw, *John Bradshaw on the Family: A New Way of Creating Solid Self Esteem* (HCI, revised 1990). See especially p.102
9. Rudyard Kipling, *Barrack Room Ballads*, First published 1898. Reprinted Dodo Press 2005.
10. Keats refers to 'A Vale of Soul Making' in a letter to George and Georgiana Keats, 21 April, 1819. In *The Letters of John Keats*, ed. H. E. Rollins, 1958, vol. 2.
11. John Gray, *Men are from Mars, Women are from Venus: The Classic Guide to Understanding the Opposite Sex* (New York: HarperCollins, 1992). John Gray has written many versions of this title.
12. Tom Brokaw, *The Greatest Generation* (New York: Random House, 1998).
13. *Twelve O'Clock High*, produced Darryl Zanuck, 1949.
14. Robert Bly, PBS interview. www.pbs.org/kued/nosafeplace/inter/bly.html
15. Stephen Crane, *The Red Badge of Courage*. (1895). Widely republished.
16. Sonia Sanchez, *Just Don't Never Give Up on Love. Callalloo*, Johns Hopkins Univ. Press, no. 20, 1984, pp.83-85.
17. Richard Lovelace, *Poems*. Widely republished.
18. Harold Bloom, *The Western Canon* (Florida: Harcourt Brace, 1994). "I think that the self, in its quest to be free and solitary, ultimately reads with one aim only: to confront greatness." p.524.
19. C. G. Jung, *Complete Works,* vol. 14, p.346. "Death is indeed a fearful piece of brutality… From another point of view, however, death appears as a joyful event. In the light of eternity it is a wedding, a *mysterium coniunctionis.* The soul attains, as it were, its missing half. It achieves wholeness."
20. Dennis Watlington, *Chasing America: Notes from a Rock'n'Soul Integrationist* (New York: Thomas Dunne Books, 2004). All quotations are from private conversations with the author August 2007.
21. The Beatles, *All You Need Is Love*. First broadcast June 25, 1967.

Chapter Eight

The Monarch Pair

The Monarch Pair is best described by comparison. If the Warrior-Lover is the image of a person who is able to be truly open, honest and vulnerable with another, then the Monarch Pair displays the same quality except extended beyond the pairing and into the whole world.

The King and Queen together represent the fusion of male and female; the decisive and accommodating; executive and nurturing; yin and yang. A king must be able to make hard decisions and live with them. Perhaps those decisions involve condemning others for the greater good of society. Criminals have to be incarcerated, perhaps executed. Virtuous citizens also have to be rewarded, and erring individuals corrected in such a way that they do not become alienated. The population must be looked after, or they'll rebel, and yet they must pay their taxes and serve the social structures or the state cannot run itself. A ruler must know when to be stern and when to be kind and, like a good parent, must occasionally show love by being tough. History is littered with examples of male leaders who were ousted because they didn't get this balance right and whether it is the Revolutionary War against King George ("No taxation without representation!") or the Reign of Terror in the French Revolution, in each case the ruler was not sufficiently alert to the needs of those who were being ruled.

The bond between ruler and ruled is, essentially, a love bond. Indeed the situation is directly comparable to what happens to most parents. Parents love each other (we hope) or at least imagine they do, and when they produce children they find they love their children, too. And yet a newborn is a lot of work. Children require love and effort and time and money in abundance, and even when grown they tend to have needs that are extensive. Grown children have their crises, need to be advised, sometimes even challenged, and occasionally their distress is such that they need to be treated as dependents again. The Monarch's situation is such that she finds it necessary to extend the lessons of love beyond the boundaries of the spousal pair.

The Challenges of the Monarch Pair

As we know, children grow up to be their own independent people. Parents will love the child and yet often will be astounded at how different a child of theirs can be from either parent. "Where did this one come from?" declared one mother, laughing at her math-obsessed kid. "I don't know where she got that from. Neither [her father] nor me has any aptitude for that," confessed a mother about her child's ability with music. As the years roll by the child may seem either more or less like the parents, and this can lead to misunderstandings. The challenge for the Monarch is to love others – no matter how different they are from us – and try to treat them all equally and nurture them all appropriately.

We all know how hard that can be; every family has favorites. Dad and Suzie are close, like the same things, and think the same way. Dad can't understand Billy, and finds him difficult. He may not enjoy his son as much as his daughter. Even though he always wanted a son who liked baseball and Billy just can't stand baseball, his task as a parent is to love both children equally and not try to shape them in ways that do not seem to be a good match for who they are. In my counseling work I come up against this exact problem again and again. Adult children do not feel they were loved, do not feel they were understood, appreciated, or noticed. The list goes on. Sometimes the underlying issue is that the parents were so caught up in their own fascination with each other that the children didn't really stand a chance of making an impact. In one family the parents were totally absorbed in arguing with each other, almost every day; they did not want to end the marriage and in fact arguing *was* the way they related best. When they were squabbling they were at least passionately engaged with each other in a way that ensured each had the other's undivided attention. It was not surprising, then, that the children felt like spectators in the family. When they grew up they moved a long way from the parents and from each other, and the possibilities for working out and correcting the emotional neglect were dramatically reduced.

The parent's duty, therefore, if she is to be a Monarch who is in herself a balance of male and female, King and Queen, is to love the children and to respect each child's autonomy because that child is an individual. The parent has to encourage each child in whatever endeavors he or she undertakes, no matter how different these may be from the parent's own values, and do so without coercive judgment. If this is allowed to happen the parent can be moved to a place of learning and even wonder that causes her to respect the child's capabilities even more. This has to happen whether or not the Monarch is in a pairing. And yet – the archetypal image is specifically paired male with female. Just as there is pressure on the king or queen to be married in any country that has a monarchy, so it seems to be the case that the archetype occurs only as part of a pairing. This does not mean that the only possible pairings are between men and women. I suspect that the archetype is telling us an important psychic truth – that in order to be at Monarch level, and to stay there, one has to have balanced the different aspects inside one's self and that this is a task best done while in an equal loving relationship with another. And here's the nub: the other person does not always have to be present. In fact the other person can be alive or long dead, a lover or a sibling or a mentor; what seems to matter is not who the person is or was, but whether the loving attachment allowed the Monarch to learn the necessary balance, internalize those qualities, and stay with them. A loving remembrance can be just as effective as a living person, and can remind us to honor and love what that person had to offer us so we can in turn respect others, especially our children. All around us we can observe examples of single parents who have achieved these qualities internally, and who live them every day.

The artist whose daughter becomes a marine biologist may never understand the fascination of algae, but may well be delighted by the devotion the child has for the subject and find personal closeness even in such differences. The classical musician whose son plays in a heavy metal band may not like the music, but can still admire the child's level of interest in the chosen field. These are all lessons in which love is asked to rise above mere preference. According to an old Jewish proverb I heard once from a rabbi, "Families are God's way of telling us that we have to love people we may not like very much."

If we keep the comparisons at the level of the family, however, we are not able to see how the Monarch is different from the Warrior-Lover. The difference is in terms of scale. The Monarch will take these familial lessons and apply them to her whole world. So the true Monarch might be the person who runs a community organization, or a company, by applying the same standards we have just witnessed within the family to those who are not part of the family, and who are in a different relationship as regards power. That is a tall order. Within the business world we can sometimes see confused posturing within companies that want to be seen as a 'family' or a 'community' that is devoted to quality. For the most part this is public relations silliness, and has nothing to do with the realties of executive privilege or the callous domination of the workforce that has become synonymous with profitability. For our purposes we have to recognize that the successful organization based in mutual understanding needs a balance of both aspects – humanity and efficiency – which is just what the Monarch has to achieve. The successful Monarch has to listen to what the subjects need. The successful company will always do much better if upper management listens to the workers who can tell them what is needed on the factory floor, and taking note of this is an important aspect of decision-making.

Other structures can give us clues here. An Army may be made up of commanders, who can be stern and even unpleasant, but the successful commander will also be loved, and this is surprisingly often the case. Commanders or leaders who are loved and respected, obeyed and cherished, tend to be those who are prepared to be open and straightforward. The enormous loyalty that some leaders are accorded does not depend upon them being remote. It depends upon whether or not those they lead feel understood, recognized, and cared for – which in any other circumstance would be called love. In return the citizens and soldiers give their devotion, and often their lives, to the tasks they are assigned to. In a demoralized army or a suffering nation the main ingredient is always the feeling that the leaders do not know or care what is happening in the day to day lives of the people, and so there is little trust, confidence, or real courage. Presidents and senators are routinely voted out of office for exactly these reasons.

To return to the Monarch parent, then, we can say that this figure has to have the skills to develop an intimate relationship with a spouse at the same time as maintaining a vital engagement with the world. If we consider this in the greater sense of the Monarch as the leader of a nation, he or she has to trust certain advisers implicitly – just as a married pair would trust each other – and yet be aware that even these advisors may have faults and incapacities. They need to be loved, respected, listened to, and their insights need to be weighed appropriately. The Monarch will also listen for the subjects' needs (just like a parent with children) and will decide what the best action should be for the good of all concerned, even if that makes a few subjects very upset. The Monarch realizes that even when everyone has been treated with respect not everyone is going to be happy with the result, and that this is just part of what happens. The Monarch learns not to take things personally. The Monarch will stand up for what is right and is prepared to deal with any moans and groans from those who feel differently, and in fact will recognize dissent as an essential part of an open process. The ego, which until now tended to be associated with a person's desire to get what she wants, is now used as an adjunct to clear judgment. It's no longer a case of being seen to be right, but of *doing* what's right.

For most of us living within a family and a community and being able to treat everyone in a respectful way means – often – putting one's own needs aside in this way. And yet "one's own needs" is the phrase we give to this, when if we care to look carefully we would have to say that the well-being of all those around us is actually our "need" as much as anything could be. The company director who deals with his workforce fairly will ensure the long-term survival of the company while training up other like-minded managers who will eventually take over. At the family level if we develop loving relationships with our children they will love us for who we are long after we have anything material to offer them, for example. And they will be the people who will help us face our declining physical health as we age. They will be the ones to whom we hand over control as we get too infirm to manage our responsibilities. They are the ones who will help us die. The Monarch's task is to be able to instruct others even during the dying process.

These days we have lawyers and trusts and binding agreements that hand most of this responsibility to strangers. Often this is a good idea and yet, in some ways it's a poor substitute for the loving bond that one could have hoped for. We've all read in the papers about families who wish, lovingly, for their ailing members to be allowed to die, only to find that this decision is not theirs anymore – it is the doctor's, or the hospital's. Laws drawn up to protect the individual do not always take account of what may be merciful and loving. How can they? People who are strangers to the particulars of each specific situation drew them up. The point that needs to be made here is that what was once an opportunity for parents to exercise trust in the gradual handing-over of power within the family has now become a function to be handled by professionals only, and that makes it harder for anyone to learn any spiritual values from it.

The death of a loved one, of course, presents all concerned with important opportunities to re-assess what life and love might be. When we die we seem not to care too much about how much money is in our savings account or how our collection of Ming vases is doing. All we seem to care about is whether we were loved in the past, whether we are loved now, and whether others can see and can feel that we love them. Since these things are hard to achieve when people are in pain, when relatives are anxious and sometimes exhausted, and when physical stamina is failing, we may need to look for guidance to existing rituals. Luckily there is considerable wisdom in some of these rituals. For example, the Catholic rite of final unction is not just about deathbed confession. It seems, rather, to be a reassurance that God loves the individual, is waiting to receive him or her, and that whatever we have done wrong no longer matters in the light of that love. It's not the only ritual for the dying, of course, but it does seem to be one of the richer ones. As such it becomes a model for what our task is as we die, and what the requirements are for those who are present at the death. Notice, final unction does not say to the dying person, "You can't go yet! We need you! Stay!!" The ritual is not about the desperation of making the living feel better by holding the sufferer back; it is about allowing the dying person to let go, in peace and in love, knowing that no more needs to be expressed.

Since most people die with some loved ones involved in the process, and since the loved ones may not know what to do or how to act (aside from feeling sorrow) the responsibility for making a good exit rests chiefly with the person who is least able to do much – the dying person. Dying is not an event that fits neatly within the six stages because it is eminently possible for someone to progress rapidly through several stages in a very short space of time when approaching death. Faced with extinction some people have shown admirable love and courage, and as a result their deaths have been a huge gift to others. A few words, spoken from the heart at the exact right moment, can have a substantial impact on another's life. One man said he felt transformed by his father's dying smile and the words, "You're a good lad." We could say the son was projecting feelings into the situation, and that would probably be true, yet it would miss the point that the father somehow knew what to say and that it needed to be said, needed to be received. The words may not find their way into the *Oxford Book of Quotations* anytime soon, but they served the necessary purpose so the son could feel truly loved and appreciated. The son was able to heal, and his ability to live an enhanced life was placed on a better footing.

The Monarch's task is to be able to instruct others, no matter what level of development they may have achieved, in how to deal with life and death and mortality successfully because the Monarch has already gained a vital awareness of what is required. To be able to use one's own death as an event that can enhance the living awareness of others is, one might say, the ultimate gift of a loving spirit.

The extensive apparatus of medical technology and complex decision making has, today, rather got in the way of us being able to see what dying is all about. In fact this experience is likely to be seen as a failure of the science and the drugs to extend the loved one's life, when we would be better placed spiritually if we were able to see the human interactions more clearly.

Points to Ponder:
Delegation

The easiest way to envision this archetype is as the person who trusts, delegates, and nurtures others – exactly as a good manager or the skilled parent will do. The Monarch does this because it is the best way to get each person to reach his or her full potential so that each can contribute to the good of the whole state. This is a way forward that demands significant risks; trust always does. But the Monarch knows that the task is not to stay in a job so much as it is to maintain balance within the kingdom. Evil will arise, and bad people will attempt unpleasant things, because that is the nature of things. The Monarch has to nurture the good so that it can cope with the bad, contain it, and even accept the inevitability of its presence. This is a larger, more impersonal love than we have seen until now, one in which evil is accepted without repugnance, but without joy either.

In The Bedroom:
Love as Sacrament

In monarchies the King and Queen are so much in the public eye that infidelity cannot remain undetected for long. We all know that monarchs throughout history have had lovers, but this isn't the highest expression of what a Monarch can be. Yet we're not talking about what tends to happen in the world. We're looking at an archetype as an image that is intended to guide us.

The Monarch in the bedroom is one who has the confidence that comes from knowing that her partner is faithful, honest, and loving. Just as sex between the king and queen is likely to produce children who will be the next generation of rulers, so sex for the Monarch is a sense that a profound and productive connection is being made, one that links each partner to the cycles of time, nature, fruition, and eventual decay. We can explain this in part by looking at the Grail legends of King Arthur: there the impotent Fisher king is a figure whose sexual incapacity is seen to bring famine and desolation to the land and he has to be healed before the kingdom can prosper again. For Oedipus the incestuous wedding to Jocasta calls down plagues upon Thebes, and the land is blighted, forcing him into exile. The person at Monarch level, in a similar way, knows that sex and sexuality are not just about personal love and attachment (although it has to be about that too), but that they mirror the larger cycles of Nature of which we are all part and of which we should all be in awe. Sex for the person at Monarch level becomes a celebration of the mysterious, the beautiful, and the passionate. At the same time the Monarch knows that he is just a person engaging in loving activity with one he loves and that they both are, ultimately, of not much cosmic importance. It's only when we can feel this fleeting quality of intense joy as we connect with one we love, blessed and tainted by our awareness that all too soon we'll be dead, that we can know, dimly, our place within the universe. The sex becomes more than sensual pleasure. It becomes an affirmation of all that is holy in love and all that is redemptive. Since all creativity comes, ultimately, from God, every time any of us is creative we echo what God is constantly doing for the world, and loving sex, of the sort we're considering here, grows more love, more connection, and perhaps even will produce a child who will be a creation, an ordinary miracle, also.

At this point the Monarch is partaking of the miraculous nature of the world. That this astonishing aspect is daily taken for granted by most of us does not make it any the less miraculous. Those who are aware of this aspect of life touch the essence of what it is to be a Magician.

Feeling the Energy of the Archetype

To contact the power of the Monarch it's only necessary to think of a time when you were in charge of something. How did you manage that? Did you work harmoniously with others, or were you imperious? Did you find the experience taught you how to get along better with others? If so, cherish that time and allow yourself to recall it in all its fullness. Some people do this by having photographs of themselves with the team they led; if you have such a photo, look carefully at that picture. Try to recall everyone in it – the good things and the less good. How was it to deal with them? What did it demand from you? What did it give you? Recalling events such as this can help us mobilize the power of the Monarch. Nowadays, group photos are frequent, plentiful, and as a result sometimes disregarded. Yet they have power if we choose to recall it and value it. If you find yourself deliberately avoiding group snapshots you may want to ask why you don't want to be identified as part of a team of workers. It may be that it's not just shyness but a real desire not to be associated with others. If so, that's fine, and you may need to consider different situations, perhaps where you mentor others, because we all have the Monarch within us, and it's not that hard to contact that energy if we wish to. After all, if we don't seek out the energy where it exists in small events, it's much harder to mobilize it fully so we can bring it to its full expression.

If you've ever experienced the pleasure of working with a partner, knowing that you were both doing a good job, it can be a truly enlightening example of what it feels like to be in the Monarch energy. Remember, though, that the tasks have to have been worthwhile, have involved substantial trust in the other person and her abilities, and the tasks will have been part of responding to others – listening, guiding, being present to their needs. My background is in teaching, and I've seen team teachers who truly seemed to work in absolute harmony with each other, and it's been an inspiration. I've also seen team teachers who simply divided up their class time using a stop-watch and who read from notes that were clearly decades old. If you have seen truly effective teamwork in action or if you've been part of it, take a moment and remember those times now; perhaps you could even write down the names, places, and times. Allow yourself to feel that time again. That's the energy.

The Monarch Pair in the Tarot

There are several cards that mirror the Monarch Pair, and they all occur together. The Hierophant, number five, is often seen as the card of society and marriage,

THE HIGH PRIESTESS

THE EMPRESS.

THE EMPEROR.

THE HIEROPHANT

which matches the worldly concerns of the Monarch with getting the right people suited to the right partners, including working partners. Until comparatively recently members of the royal courts of Europe could not marry unless the monarch agreed to it, and in certain families the father's permission had to be sought before the happy couple could head off to the altar. Similarly, military and civil appointments were all made with the Monarch's approval. This card therefore seems to express the worldly aspect of the Monarch as the regulator of a functioning social system.

Numbers three and four are the Empress and Emperor. Notice it is the Empress that has the higher status since its lower number places it above the emperor in the sequence. In the cards, The Empress is shown relaxing on a comfortable seat, out of doors, while the Emperor is on his throne, clasping his scepter and orb, clearly in charge of worldly things and looking very official. One could hardly ask for a better version of the Monarch Pair in terms of their stereotypically contrasting attributes. Yet notice that it is the female qualities of gentleness and love that take precedence.

The next high card as we move up the numerical values is also female, The High Priestess, number two. She mirrors the usually male Hierophant, since she too sits between two pillars in a very similar pose, but where the Hierophant has two kneeling monks at his feet, the High Priestess has the crescent moon, sacred to Diana the virgin goddess, at her feet, and the pillars she sits between are contrasted: one is white and one is black. Behind her is a tapestry showing ripe figs or pomegranates splitting open, with their obviously sexual reference to the vagina. The High Priestess in some cultures was actually higher ranked than the ruler. The priestesses at the oracle in Delphi had little in the way of temporal power for example, but kings would seek their advice before undertaking decisive actions and defer to their suggestions. The High Priestess is a figure who can unite others with the Divine.

These four cards together seem to indicate the balance of temporal and spiritual power that the Monarch Pair can achieve at its highest level, and this is depicted as a series of steps of which the High Priestess is the top most. This is a richly suggestive set of images and one cannot ignore the close correspondences they share with this archetypal stage.

The Monarch in the Real World

One of the more obvious examples of the Monarch in our world would have to be Oprah Winfrey. As we all know she rose from a difficult past to head her own TV company, and having done so she now uses that power and influence to bring out the best in others. Her school for girls in South Africa took a huge mount of money and time to set up, and she took on this project deliberately because she recognized that if the country was to nurture the leadership potential of its citizens, then it would need to invest in the gifts of those who had been until now disempowered and ignored – the women. Oprah set herself to change the obvious imbalances of a society that was in crisis, and she did so by thinking clearly about what was practical, possible, and logical. Her style is Monarchical in the sense that she does not personally do all the work. Instead she sought out the best advice, listened to others, weighed the situation, and facilitated its growth. She is an inspiring high level administrator – she knows when to hand over authority to those she trusts. She is compassionate and also decisive, a balance of the two sides of this archetype that need to operate in harmony. That's the Monarch as visionary manager.

Oprah has been criticized by many and she's also been adored by far more people because she's obviously trying to move everyone to a higher level of functional awareness. Her aim is for the world to be a better place, although she is careful not to attach to a specific personal vision. She doesn't say, 'I want it this way!' Instead she seems to ask how things could be made better and then she lets the situation unfold as it needs to in response to living circumstances. The fixed vision of how things 'should' be is the mark of the person who is not prepared to listen or accept another's views. Such a vision ceases to be alive or open to growth, and becomes merely a fixation. Oprah knows better than that. She has an overall vision and seeks to discover how it will unfold in all its ramifications. By contrast, George Bush had an ego-fuelled vision of himself as the victorious president who conquered Iraq – but it seems evident he had absolutely no idea as to what that might involve in the long term. We are currently paying the price for his fixed and inadequate vision that had everything to do with image and little to do with substance. That is a ghastly parody of the Monarch's methods.

If we look at Oprah as a successful Monarch what we'll see is that she can help real miracles of change to happen and so at times she will be identifiable as a Magician. Yet it's worth making the distinction here because Oprah is very much based in aiding those who can then continue to make things better for themselves independently. Her emphasis is on the here and now, in righting obvious wrongs, and not on the relationship each of us may have to an awareness of the Divine. That's where the Monarch stops and the Magician takes over.

What we may need to be aware of, also, is that the Monarch can appear even when we may have given up hope for that figure. Let's look again at Bill Clinton. He may still be dogged by his less than admirable reputation, yet his new book *Giving* is remarkable because he suggests that we are here on earth to make a positive difference, and then he proceeds to give examples of people who have done this when one might not have expected it of them. He includes activists for charitable humanitarian causes at all levels of income; Dr. Paul Farmer appears alongside Bill Gates, for example. He honors their diverse achievements at the same time as he suggests that their examples are available to us so that we can be more like them. In this way Clinton is choosing to describe examples of effective action and to inspire others – and so he hands power back to people. It took courage for him to do this, knowing how many cynics would be prepared to laugh because of his former misdeeds. It takes an evolved soul to be able to move past mistakes.

Using Oprah, Clinton, and others as examples we can identify additional Monarchs around us, although there will be many who achieve Monarch status on a smaller scale than those I've mentioned, and who will probably go unnoticed. I encourage you to look around our world and ask where the real Monarchs are. If we can identify that potential within our leaders I think we'll be less likely to make mistakes at the ballot box and the voting machine. We'll also be able to identify those figures in the public media who aren't Monarchs – those who have used their elevated positions in ways that have spread sadness or encouraged us to think in negative ways. These are the people to avoid. Many of the talk shows we've had paraded before us in past years have probably been entertaining after a fashion, but some have also encouraged us to think less of our fellow citizens, and some have been demeaning. Jerry Springer's show that featured college students who were stranded on spring break without money, and who would do anything to get the cash he was offering, struck me as not so much reality TV as humiliation TV. No one becomes a bigger soul under those circumstances.

Notes

1. William Clinton, *Giving: How Each of Us Can Change the World* (New York: Knopf, 2007). Notice how the title directly addresses the sense of people empowering themselves to make change occur.

Chapter Nine

The Magician

❦

If it seems that the Monarch has managed to get everything squared away neatly – romance, lasting love and attachments to children – then where does the Magician come in? This most elusive archetype is in some ways only available for observation at the moments when the magic is actually being done, and sometimes not even then. Better still is that the Magician can arise at almost any of the six stages, even if only temporarily.

In order to be fully Magicians we must let go of everything to do with status, the ego and pride. When we do that we are able to speak our truth without guile, without expecting to be rewarded for what we say, and we do so because that is an act of love in itself. Falsehood is never loving and is only ever present when we're trying to salvage some pride or some goodwill to soothe our own egos. The challenge is to speak our truth simply because it is the truth as we feel it. And the most important truth is the one we knew at infancy and lost as we began to develop ego-awareness: it is that we are loving beings. Remember the baby? It loves; that's what it does. We may rationalize that away by saying it is acting instinctually and that would be correct. The baby knows *only* love. As it insists on being itself and loving others, we find that others begin to experience fierce love in return. Custody battles are about many things, yet many of them are also about the primary bond that parents both have with the children.

The task of the Magician is to relearn that love; that unblended straightforward devotion and trust that the Innocent has. Earlier we called it "God-love" because it's so strong and pure it seems to come from another dimension entirely. The Magician's task is to be open and regain that innocence, bringing it back into the world fearlessly. The world we presently have is one that is dominated by the ego-principle and as such it will ridicule the Innocent-Magician's entire lack of agenda about such things. The Magician wants to bring more love into the world so that people can work together in harmony for ends that have nothing to do with personal wealth and everything to do with loving stewardship of all people on the earth. There's no need for personal gain because until we all win, no one can really feel like a winner. For example, to win anything – a better job, a better standard of living – at the expense of someone else feeling like a loser is a hollow victory indeed. To get rich by polluting the planet is merely being a slave to ego insecurities that value money more than what is right and good. On the other hand to remove pollution from the planet is to enrich everyone upon it, far into the future, and that has very little to do with personal gratifications of a material sort. What could be more loving?

The Challenges of the Magician:
Detachment

The Magician's situation in love is to rise to a condition of acceptance at a new level – one of detachment. It's hard to describe, and perhaps only poets have been able to do it. Leonard Cohen is particularly quotable, but not because he was talking specifically about love: he was talking about poetry, which is his way of loving the world. Interviewed in the movie *I'm Your Man* he had interesting things to say about his Zen teacher Roshi who, he said, "Deeply cared, or perhaps he deeply didn't care, who I was." The point jumps out at us. We don't love people because of what they've done, how they look, or how famous they are. We love the core of them and that means *allowing them to be whoever they are, and still loving them.*

In terms of personal creativity, Cohen goes on to say of his writing: "You abandon your masterpiece and then you slip into the real masterpiece." It's a sentiment he repeats in another of his songs: "You lose your grip / and then you slip / Into the Masterpiece." The grip is surely the ego desire we all have to create something wonderful, or be someone special, when the point is that we are all valuable already, because we are all worthy of respect. But we can't reach that knowledge until we let go of the hunger to be rewarded in that way. When we let go of ego then real creative power will take us where it needs to go. The song sings and the story tells itself – but sometimes we have to get out of our own way first. We do not make the Masterpiece; it already exists, and we slip into it as we slip into an awareness of that greatest of all masterpieces, existence.

For the Monarch to become a Magician she has to accept that it's necessary to stop trying to achieve, and just when we stop trying (the bugbear of the Warrior) we let the energy of the universe, God energy, work through us. That's when marvelous things can happen, as Cohen acknowledges. The Monarch's ultimate challenge is to let go – and become a Magician. This is what Shakespeare's Prospero did in the *The Tempest*. He let go of control and trusted in love, and he is in many ways just the clearest expression of this tendency, which exists in so many of Shakespeare's plays. As Cohen says, "It gets easier when you stop expecting to win." When we give up this idea that we have to win, be the best and feed that fragile ego – that's when we can truly become more fully ourselves. Life is, after all, a long defeat; we get old and tired and our knees hurt. We have success but never quite enough. And if we stay in that place of restlessness and wanting we will surely become unhappy. Others will be able to love us fully only when we stop trying to be victorious, or better, or right, and when we do that we free ourselves to be able to love freely and to be loved. It's a tough task for a king, since the job demands that the Monarch remains in control, enforces respect, and keeps the kingdom well regulated. If the Monarch stays with these temporal duties – which after all are what she's expected to do – it can be very difficult to make the full transition to Magician level.

Perhaps the most direct way to describe this is that the Monarch feels that she must function as an effective human being, so she feels herself to be a human who is moving towards a spiritual experience. The Magician knows she is a spiritual being who is having a human experience.

Consider that for a moment. Think how our attitudes would change if we were to try to live that way. As humans we love each other and we are aware also that we are all fragile, we will grow old and die, and that love is threatened by the ravages of time. Here's an example that may help. One of my students described the happiness she felt with her husband as they moved into their late seventies: "It's so wonderful. We sit and hold hands and we can't believe how good it feels, and at the same time we're sad that it took so long to get to this. Because we don't have that many years left." That is a poignant example of a human experience that approaches the spiritual. And yet this is all altered if we think of ourselves as spiritual beings who are being granted the gift of a human experience. The emotions we feel in this human experience then become our instructors, telling us about the larger truths that continue to exist when human limitations are removed. When we focus on the quality of the love shared by those two older people, in that moment, rather than thinking about how sad it is that they met each other so late in life, we can be profoundly glad, inspired that the love they feel emerged to show us its marvelous richness. And when we do that we forget all the years of searching for love, because we witness the achieved love in all its fullness.

It takes us back to the parables of Jesus. He described the kingdom of heaven as being like a man who hires workers for his vineyard throughout the course of a long day, and at the end pays them all the same. In human terms that's wrong. The Union officials would be all over that. In divine terms, if the reward is heaven, it doesn't matter how long or how short one's apprenticeship is, because the reward itself is much more important than how long it took to earn it. If I buy just one lottery ticket and win the jackpot I'm delighted. If I buy three tickets a week for five years and then win I'd be an idiot if I turned around and complained about all the non-winning tickets. If I go out on fruitless dates for ten years before I meet the love of my life I'd be foolish to reproach my beloved with having wasted my time for so long. I'd be much better off enjoying the love that has now arrived. The Magician focuses on what is important and lets the mistakes go. The Magician always focuses on the good.

Points to Ponder

If the Magician seems rather daunting, it's worth spelling out that the archetype is only an *image* of what we can aspire to in terms of our family, friends, and those close to us. Few of us are able to be fully present to people all the time, to be open, accepting, non-judgmental and yet intensely aware of who this person *is* – though I suppose a few priests, saints, and a very few therapists can manage that consciousness. In fact, the therapist has an easier job, since a client rarely comes to the appointment with more than one other person, unless we're considering family or group therapy. So we can see that the comparisons to the family that we've been making throughout in no way belittle the demands on the person who goes through the six stages of development – in fact it seems to represent the most demanding version available.

If we are to understand what the Magician does we will have to see it from the point of view of what it feels like to meet such a person. Ram Dass, describing the first meeting with his guru Maharaji, seems to outline the way a Magician works with some succinctness. When he met the guru, Maharaji told him what he, Ram Dass had been thinking the previous evening, in effect reading his mind. Ram Dass's reaction is worth quoting.

> I felt this extremely violent pain in my chest and a tremendous wrenching feeling and I started to cry. And I cried and I cried and I cried. And I wasn't happy and I wasn't sad. It was not that kind of crying. The only thing I could say was it felt like I was home. Like the Journey was over. Like I had finished.

When we encounter the Magician, the magic happens inside us and it's not always comfortable. What Ram Dass seems to be describing is the moment of relief that we feel when all our longings are recognized by another and are validated. Our innermost self has been seen, and accepted, and we realize that we are in fact divine creatures, linked through spirit in ways we had not previously acknowledged. It's a totally different way of being, and it is completely unlike any other definition of love.

Ram Dass, again, trying to describe how Maharaji worked his magic says that the surprising thing to him was that the guru didn't make plans, or draw up schemes or convene committees.

He will walk to a place and there will be a saint who has lived in that place or cave and he'll say, 'There will be a temple here,' and then they build a temple. And they do all this around Maharaji. He appears to do nothing.

The Magician seems to do nothing and yet achieves everything. *The Tao Te Ching* puts it this way:

> When the Master governs, the people
> Are hardly aware he exists.

And again:

> The Master doesn't talk, he acts.
> When his work is done
> The people say, 'Amazing:
> We did it all by ourselves!'

Surely the best ruler is the one who is able to motivate others to be the best people they can be? And in that sense they govern themselves.

In this way the Magician has to contact the real power of love, forgiveness and acceptance that we saw first in the Innocent. We've already noted that the Innocent comes back to refuel the Warrior-Lover as the Warrior learns to trust and love another person implicitly. This is the first step. At the Monarch level this sense of trust is extended so that it encompasses most of the people who make the kingdom work. A Monarch has to retain a certain amount of canny suspicion, however, or risk running into trouble with rebellious or greedy subjects. For the Magician the task is much greater still. The Magician has to have total faith in the divine goodness of all aspects of creation, and must love everyone, trusting that even the evil aspects of the world will eventually be turned to good. That sounds impossible and unrealistic, though we have only to look at what Jesus went through to recognize that it may well be impossible for most of us to understand fully. But that should in no way stop us from trying.

In the Bedroom

In some ways it is almost unnecessary to consider the Magician in the bedroom, since the power of the love this archetype connects to goes beyond the merely sexual. The Magician's focus is on the spiritual, not the physical, so one could say that when this figure is sexual it is as a Monarch and not as a Magician, since sex is firmly located in the physical world. This leads inevitably to confusion, since few if any of us can be permanently at the level of the Magician, yet we expect our Magician figures to be beyond sex. Catholic priests are supposed to be celibate, but as we all are aware, many are not. Similarly some of the recent Indian gurus have been exposed as sexual predators and Bhagwhan Shree Rajneesh springs to mind as having been on the receiving end of such accusations. What perhaps should surprise us is the shock with which the general public has reacted. We seem to want our Magicians to be permanently at Magician level and that may not be possible. There is no excuse for sexual exploitation, of course, yet we can understand such behaviors as examples of how the Magician will inevitably need to return to a less exalted level of existence for large portions of time.

When the Magician is acting as a full Magician, he or she doesn't have sex so much as becomes a truly loving presence – and that goes way beyond sex.

Understanding the Energy of the Archetype

The experience of the Magician is readily available to us all, although we may need to be aware that it exists for most of us only in flashes. Can you recall an occasion where you spoke and the words seemed to come by themselves? How did that feel? I'm not talking about occasions, which I'm sure we've all had, when we've blurted out the exact wrong thing or been angry and hurtful. I'm asking you to recall moments when you said or did something that was exactly the right thing, even though you didn't know it until later. One man recalled how he suddenly felt he needed to hold on to a child sitting next to him in a car just moments before the door inexplicably flew open. He was as surprised as anyone, but the child's life was saved. When I worked with disturbed adolescents my director, Peter Riach, described how he was standing near two young men who were talking together, and he suddenly felt he had to step between them. He had no reason for doing so, but he walked forward. The very second he did so he was able to catch and hold one of the young men, who had lunged forward and would otherwise have stabbed the other. A modest man, Peter didn't try to claim he'd foreseen the event. He knew he'd been lucky enough to listen to the inner promptings of his whole being, and that it was an example of the Magician at work.

A different example might be those moments when you stopped trying, and let things take their course. Has that ever happened to you? The phrase, 'Let go, let God' comes to mind, and sometimes it really does feel as if God has been waiting for us to stop trying to control things. Russell Baker recalls in his memoir that he was so terrified of his flying instructor and that he had such an awful hangover the day of his final examination that he stopped caring how well he flew. He just got in and flew the plane; he turned in an almost perfect score. He really had got out of his own way that day. Have you ever had any experiences like that? If so, cherish them, because it may be that this was the Magician in you emerging.

A teacher friend of mine relates how he was trying to get through the syllabus with his class, and they were resisting every inch of the way. So one day he walked in and didn't even bring his books, and he asked the class what was going on, how they felt about things. He did so in a loving way, almost as an Innocent, expecting them to be pretty negative and instead they responded to his openness, speaking thoughtfully. They worked through what they felt was going on while he listened, learned, and saw them in a new way. The class changed from that day on. It still had occasional problems, but now they all knew how to solve them as they arose and the students were able to deal with the resistances and difficulties for themselves. Retelling the story the man had tears in his eyes, and he knew he really loved 'that bunch of clowns' as he called them. He'd learned about the right way to let go without it being a case of giving up. That's the Magician at work – and sometimes the Magician can only emerge when we've tried everything else (there's that 'trying' again) and we feel we have nothing left to lose.

As with all the stages, we need to remind ourselves that we can contact them, and we have to do so regularly because we forget. The process can never be cerebral. It's not enough to say to ourselves that we did it once upon a time, because like any physical activity we need to practice it. We have to reconnect with the emotions felt *at the time* and truly feel them again. That's the way to know the energy of the archetype and invite it to enter more into our lives. And it is perhaps only when we recall this that we can see that it is not so much a case of us achieving the archetype's level by some effort of our own, but rather of the archetype being able to work through us as we access our deep wisdom. When we allow this to happen it is always a loving action. It's only when we're trying for some desired result that we assume we can know what is 'best', and that's when we miss the mark. It is at Magician stage that we can understand the energy of love by respecting it and giving it space to operate. What we discover, of course, is that the archetype of the Magician is made up of the very best of all the previous five stages.

The Magician in the Tarot:
the Completion of the Major Arcana's Cycle

The Magician in the Tarot deck is the highest card of all. It shows the Magician performing some type of religious rite, while before him (it seems to be a male figure) are the four symbols of the rest of the pack: pentacles, swords, staves, and cups. He is actually at that moment working magic – or rather he is allowing magic to happen by connecting to the energy of the Universe and allowing it to

THE MAGICIAN.

flow through him. He reveres that energy so much that he has suppressed his ego and any selfish desires to be better than anyone else and has instead become the willing servant of the primary creative energy, which is in itself love. Over his head is the sign for infinity, rather than a halo. It marks this as the most powerful and all-inclusive of the stages; one hand holds a rod aloft and the other points down, as he links the higher and lower realms. The figure is a young man, not a gray-bearded wizard, symbolizing the eternally revivifying power of the connection to the divine. Red roses (symbols of passion) and white lilies (symbols of purity) are massed before him showing the twin aspects of love, sexual and platonic, and favoring neither above the other.

The symbols spread before him on the altar are likewise important reminders of the Magician's role. Since the pentacle (or pentangle) is the sign of the planet Venus, we can see it as symbolic of the female principle. Swords are, likewise, symbolic of the male and the phallus – there's Mars and Venus again – and both of these symbols are echoed in cups and staves. The pentacle and the sword are the sorts of symbols one might call elevated – swords existed in wealthy families and the pentacle was an abstract – while cups and staves were once common even in the poorest home. So the Magician can be seen as gathering all kinds of male and female symbols together from both high and low social levels, which is a beautiful way to hint at the completion of the balance that must be achieved for the Warrior-Lover and the Monarch, and which must be maintained by the Magician.

If this all seems tenuous I would point out that for most of us visual images stay in the mind far longer than written descriptions or analyses. The Tarot's rich imagery is utterly memorable and seems to encompass all the points we have been considering. We can use the cards, therefore, as reminders and when we temporarily forget what we are supposed to do in our lives, we can be refreshed by images that are not intended to be diagnostic so much as evocative. The power of the image has always been honored in religious instruction of all kinds for exactly that reason, from the magnificent stained glass windows of the medieval cathedrals to the temple sculptures at Khajuraho in India.

The Full Spread of the Major Arcana

The entire spread of Tarot cards can be seen, now, as a pictorial diagram of some of the mileposts of development that we can expect to encounter as we progress through the six stages. Seeing this, we can conclude that the Tarot may have, amongst its many uses, a role in helping people to visualize their life trajectories, and perhaps it can guide us similarly.

Using the Rider pack we can spread the major Arcana cards out in their numerical order. What we'll see is, as we've already mentioned, that there seem to be cards that are paired and some that stand alone. Here is how one can arrange them in numerical order, with the lines separating the different archetypes.

Those who know the Tarot will already have noticed that of all the decks available we have been discussing only the Rider-Waite Tarot. This deck is regarded by many as the classic authoritative Tarot and was certainly highly regarded by Joseph Campbell. Speaking with his long term friends the interviewers Michael and Justine Toms of New Dimensions Media, he insisted that it was the only reliable deck, and that all others were derivative or merely decorative. Campbell was clearly aware that the images on the cards were not random but specific, if stylized, renditions of important psychic information. It's a persuasive reason to focus first of all on the images in this deck, although of course it doesn't exclude other versions.

The Magician

The Monarch Pair

The Warrior-Lover

THE HERMIT.

WHEEL of FORTUNE.

JUSTICE.

THE HANGED MAN.

DEATH.

TEMPERANCE.

THE DEVIL.

Orphan

THE TOWER.

THE STAR.

THE MOON.

The Innocent

THE SUN.

JUDGEMENT.

THE FOOL.

THE WORLD.

At the risk of over-simplifying, it is possible to see that there is a pattern here that can be helpful. It'll be necessary to repeat some of the information we've seen in previous chapters, but only for the sake of clarity. Starting with the lowest division, if we take The Sun as the equivalent of the Innocent in its strongest expression, we can see The Fool as the version of the Innocent that has lost its way, wandering helplessly towards the cliff edge in the picture. Fools and children speak the truth according to the old proverb, and the link exists in English where 'fool' could even be a term of endearment to a child, as evidenced in Shakespeare's plays. These two cards are the balanced and unbalanced aspects of the Innocent and what separates them is the sense of the nature of this world (The World) and an awareness of the next world (the Final Judgment). It is as if the Innocent has to come to a place of understanding in which the ways of the physical world are honored in the here and now, and also the sense of eternity that instructs the child that she possesses a soul. The Fool, or the mental incompetent, cannot differentiate in this way. So we have the two aspects of this stage before us, together with the lessons that have to be learned. The placing of The Fool at the bottom of the pack is deliberate, too: in this way it stands as the opposite of The Magician. Yet we all know that the card that is The Fool is also to be seen as signifying the one who can prophesy, because he is not fully in this world and has connections to the other unseen world. The qualities of openness and innocence are precisely those that allow this to happen.

When we reach The Tower, The Star, and The Moon we'll notice that a theme of homelessness seems to be in each, and we could say that the Orphan archetype is depicted in two aspects as well as the main, balanced aspect. The Orphan's reliance on The Tower leads to a violent overthrow – suggesting the spiritual death and ultimate catastrophic disappointment of those who trust in wealth only. The Moon card suggests a mournful sense of being exiled and being unable to find a home, or to take on a spiritual path at all. There is, after all, nothing so forlorn as a lost dog. As a symbol that reflects the Orphan's tendency to attach too readily to any available home or leader, it is poignant. Between these two cards is the enigmatic figure called The Star, with two water jugs, pouring one into the pool and one onto the dry earth. Stars are more reliable as navigational guides than the sun or the moon, but they also shift around the heavens. Interestingly the card has seven stars and a main, bright star upon it. Are these the seven stars of *Ursa Major* (that easily identifiable constellation that points out the Pole Star) the one reliable guide that does not shift? Unfortunately the figure in this card is not looking at the star but at the water, perhaps even in a Narcissus-like way, intent on this odd activity of pouring water into water with one hand and with the other hand, at which she is not looking, pouring out water onto the soil. Perhaps the suggestion is of pleasant but wasted, directionless activity. The figure seems contented compared to the dog and the wolf on The Star card and the tumbling king and queen on The Tower card. Yet the figure seems curiously self-involved and ineffective, a version of the Orphan, happily settled into a routine, and this is exactly the sort of thing that can seduce us all.

Above these cards are Death, Temperance, and The Devil. We can see these as the lessons that await those of us who decide to move out of Orphan phase, or perhaps as the sort of encounters that can force us out of Orphan contentment, since they are also lessons that if left unlearned will keep us in Orphan phase. Notice that The Devil has a man and woman, naked, chained in front of him. The Orphan can always hide in a co-dependent relationship and thus not have to learn the lessons of the Temperance card, which is balance in all things. Moreover it is the fear of death, and of change, that the Death card symbolizes that will stop us using our intelligence. The Orphan may want to 'live after death' by giving the family business to a favored child, or may labor to create a 'life work' that may not mean anything to anyone else. These are important temptations that need to be understood, assimilated, and balanced by Temperance. Notice that Temperance has one foot in the water and one foot on the ground, and is pouring water from one cup to another. In this she resembles the female figure of The Star, who also has one foot on the earth and the other in the water, and is doing a very similar action. It is as if the kneeling figure in The Star is now the standing, winged, figure of Temperance.

Interestingly, it is also true to say that encounters with death and with personal disaster, which may here be conveyed by the figure of the Devil, can be the prompting any of us needs in order to force us out of the comfort of Orphan phase. Brushes with death and disaster have a way of getting people to ask serious questions about what their lives mean, and how they see their future. Sometimes this is merely a brief phase; sometimes it signals a profound shift of consciousness that sends the individual on the path of the Pilgrim. When disasters happen to us we can choose to learn the lessons and move on, or we can choose to be enslaved by the past and wallow in the role of the victim. Perhaps the Devil card, with his chained man and woman, is there to remind us of this self-imposed servitude.

Above these three cards is another triad: Wheel of Fortune, Justice, and The Hanged Man. These cards also represent lessons that need to be encountered as the individual makes the spiritual journey towards love, although they are lessons that have to be re-encountered at each stage, just as the lessons of Death, Temperance and The Devil will pop up again for the Pilgrim, the Warrior-Lover, and the Monarch. The cards, however, seem to outline the tasks ahead rather than specify precisely when they will appear. And, as most of us are aware, one doesn't deal with issues like death and justice just once in life; they keep coming back to us, in forms ever more complex than the first time; and each time we learn new lessons at a deeper level. And so we see that the lesson that here revolves around the figure of Justice seems to be one that has to do with Fate. The Wheel of Fortune can cause one to rise quickly, and also to fall in the same way, which is perhaps what the Hanged Man warns us of. Suspended upside down, perhaps dead, his dependence upon luck has not served him well. Between these two is Justice – but what sort of justice? Is it simply the law? Or is it something more transcendent? And that's the point: will we put our faith in earthly justice – as Orphans bent upon revenge will – or do we look for the true nature of justice in its merciful aspects? And how will we react when our luck fails us, something the other two cards appear to indicate? It seems we all feel at one time or another that we have been deserted by good fortune.

The Hermit must also address these questions. Notice how he looks down, seemingly more interested in inner thoughts than in the way ahead. The Pilgrim's search is one that demands these questions be weighed (notice the scales are in the hands of the Justice figure). The Warrior-Lover and the Monarch, obviously, will face the same lessons, but we could say that thinking about them has to begin here.

Above the Hermit is the card called Strength. This is one way to describe the attributes that can and must emerge in The Pilgrim and which will cause her to become a Warrior-Lover. The woman on the card is taming a male lion, and so she represents the ascendancy of compassion, intelligence, and love over sheer power. Again, the card emphasizes a balance between these aspects of intelligence and power, not just the suppression of one of them. Strength therefore could be taken to mean courage, determination, direction, attachment, love … many of the values that the Warrior-Lover seeks to embody. And when we look at the victorious soldier in The Chariot he is numerically right beside the card called The Lovers. Notice that The Lovers is the higher card, and this seems to indicate the role love will have from this point onwards. It will be stronger than mere force and will therefore balance its excesses.

As I've already commented on the next series of cards (in Chapter 8), I don't need to repeat all the information here. I'll just observe that the Hierophant is male, a symbol of earthly marriage, while above him is the female High Priestess, who suggests the higher value of spiritual communion. Between them stand the Empress and Emperor. Like all temporal rulers, the demands of everyday ruling may temporarily blind them to the spiritual aspect of what their lives could be. The loving female figure of the Priestess is their teacher and their lesson. It seems to suggest that we must all behave as if everything we do matters, not just today and with those who are around us, but always and in front of everyone. Our daily actions must be seen as partaking of holiness. How much more difficult this must be for the Monarch! There can be no shortcuts, the Priestess seems to remind us, and no more 'Oh, it won't matter this once' ways of thinking. We can no longer do things hoping no one will notice our sloppiness. Our actions must be deliberate, thoughtful, and done with a sense of holiness and reverence. The ruler must be able to say something and mean it – or his word is not going to be respected. A law is not enacted just for the need of the moment, but for the future benefit of all, we hope.

If we take this to a higher level the sense of holiness would, one hopes, include respect for all citizens and for the earth itself. How would this work? Can you imagine factories designed specifically not to pollute? Or work places organized to put the worker's needs before profitability? I'm always surprised when I mention these possibilities at how many people are eager to say, 'Impossible! It can't happen!' And it *is* absolutely impossible for those who have that mindset; but that doesn't mean it can't be done. Any society that can send space probes to Mars and Jupiter could make a dent in domestic problems if it chose to. Any society that really loved its citizens would try. The High Priestess is a reminder of the spiritual and the humanitarian demands of rule.

The Magician is the highest card and The Fool is the card with no number at all – from which conventional packs of playing cards derive the Joker. Sometimes the Magician can look like a Fool, because she is seemingly an impractical visionary. If we gaze at the cards we can see that The Fool is careless, walking towards a precipice while in the mountains. The same contrast of lofty and low is present in The Magician, except it exists in the hand gestures, pointing up and down, including all creation. The images suggest that even though The Fool has values to show us, it is only at The Magician stage that these free-floating insights can become disciplined enough to be useful. Just similarly the Innocent's love has to be reclaimed in full by the Magician – and used in a way that is productive for all.

The Tarot's origins are distant and cloudy. What I wish to show is that it shares striking correspondences with the six archetypal stages we've been looking at. It seems likely that both the Tarot and the six archetypes are drawn from a common source, the deep unconscious reservoir of the psyche, and that is why they echo down the centuries in literature and folk tales, as I demonstrated in *Stories We Need to Know*. The Tarot probably came into something like its present form around the year 1200, which is about the time that literature began to be written down in Europe as the oral tradition gave way to a more literary tradition. We could say that both forms came into physical existence at roughly the same time, although what was written down in each case certainly existed for quite some time before hand. The Tarot's advantage is that, seen in this light, its visual images work on the imagination in the same way that the characters and events of literature and stories remain memorable to us. It is hard to forget some of these pictures, and some of these tales. In a world that was largely pre-literate, the power of images and stories was indeed impressive in a way that we may not fully be able to recapture today. We can, however, still learn from them.

Notes

1. Leonard Cohen, *I'm Your Man,* directed by Lian Lunson, 2006.
2. The parable of the men hired for the vineyard is in Matthew 20: 1-16.
3. Ram Dass, *Be Here Now* (New Mexico: Lama Foundation, 1971). There are no page numbers in this book.
4. *Tao Te Ching,* trans. Steven Mitchell (New York: HarperPerennial, 1988), section 17.
5. Russell Baker, *Growing Up* (New York: Signet, 1992).
6. When King Lear says in the last scene of the play 'and my poor fool is hang'd' (5.iii. 305) commentators are divided as to whether he is talking about his court jester or his daughter Ophelia. Since he hasn't mentioned his jester for some time, and has just carried in Ophelia's body, it's more likely he's referring to her.

Chapter Ten

Courage and Love

It's clear that the Magician's attitude takes a certain type of sustained courage and faith in the decent qualities of others. This is a very different sort of courage from the Warrior-Lover's personally based certitude, of course, which seeks a specific task. We can see, therefore, that one of the attributes that has been growing through the six stages is what we have come to call courage, for want of a better term. Courage, as we have seen with the Warrior-Lover, is the quality of being able to declare one's values and stick to them even when challenged. As such, courage requires that we face our fears and move through them anyway. Let's just take a moment to look at this a little closer.

Courage has to begin somewhere, and it is the Innocent's sense of confidence in a loving world that allows the child to explore and not be fearful. It is always love that allows a child to be confident and so to grow her sense of courage. Without that initial love it could not exist. The frightened child will not leave her mother's arms, and every parent knows how important and how nerve- wracking it can be to nurture a child's sense of healthy curiosity. The Orphan, by contrast, feels a lack of love in a dangerous world and decides to live life cautiously, so personal courage is subsumed into the idea of what is acceptable. Yet the confident explorer who was once the well-adjusted Innocent can re-emerge in the Pilgrim's desire to find meaning that she can believe. Courage can be seen to grow again after being in hiding for some time.

This is important. Bravery that is based in ignorance or stupidity is only going to cause trouble. The word 'foolhardy' sums it up beautifully. Real courage has to be learned as one faces fear and agrees to struggle to overcome it. That takes an effort of will.

When the Warrior meets with her life-partner or life-cause (and so becomes a full Warrior-Lover) there is often a sense of *deciding* to commit to the cause or to the other person even if it isn't quite in the plans, even if it's not convenient. "There never seemed any option," said one woman. "I knew …" said another, and a man described it as, "I knew I had to marry her … I had to." The earlier archetypes by comparison resist love until it suits their other plans. The Warrior-Lover breaks away from the beliefs of others and asserts self-belief and faith in love itself. Therefore it is only in love that the Warrior takes up her full courage. This courage is based in accepting the risk, the freedom to make mistakes, to fail, and to do it while playing for high stakes.

To understand this it's useful to take another look at the way the Orphan tends to function. The Orphan, timid of asserting her true self, has more faith in the accepted standards of others, and tends to go for outer trappings that others agree are attractive – sometimes at the expense of the inner sense of delight that is such a vital component of the relationship with the lover. The Orphan will tend to want to think in the terms of *Cosmopolitan* or other such magazines: if I'm really good in bed this lover will stay. So the "how to" manuals are likely to be in evidence and Orphans will sometimes feel the need to practice on available 'easy' partners because they need a safe – or uncomplicated – place to do the small amount of exploring they can allow themselves. Orphans are just a little too afraid to do any real exploration of sex and sexuality, let alone love. *Victoria's Secret* lingerie and mildly racy videos might be as much as they can manage with their partner, although extra-marital affairs will be evident too. Think about that for a second. The attraction of an affair is that one can have sex, feel relatively satisfied, and do so without having to get truly close to the other person, since one is already with one's spouse. Affairs, therefore, give a veil of unreality to both relationships, since one is not fully engaged in either. The holiday romance, the fling, or the stopgap lover – all these are ways of not allowing oneself to be truly intimate with the other.

The disadvantage to this is that an affair often represents a refusal to sort out an existing situation between the original partners. What the individual who embarks on an affair is signaling is that he or she hasn't the resources to deal with the pre-existing situation fully, and hasn't the courage to admit it. Love withers because of a lack of courage, for difficulties within partnerships are always opportunities for more understanding and growth. The difficulties may in the end prove too great for the relationship, but that matters less than that the two people continue to supply each other with love and support during a time of uncertainty. Walking away from a situation does not allow anything to change for the better – after all, if one walks away then how can one truly assess what happened? Walking away is the negation that there is anything to understand and process. It allows us to feel that we haven't done anything wrong. As such it is a way to avoid using the real courage necessary to look at a life situation with honesty. And so the couple parts, and love gets lost when it could have been grown. Orphans tend to do this. They aren't really interested in much growth; they're interested in comfort and fitting in. What's behind this is a failure of courage, and without real courage, what chance has love got?

Pilgrims, on the other hand, may look for sexual partners who are older, more experienced, and even seem like risky propositions. The Pilgrim needs a teacher, a guru – even though the role of any teacher is to become obsolete eventually. We can see this when a younger woman marries an older man, finds her way in the world, and then decides she has to leave. The man may have thought his years, his status, even his wealth, would "tame" the woman. He wanted an Orphan; what he actually got was a Pilgrim, and once an emotional Pilgrim has found her courage she won't be content with second best. She may stay in the marriage but move her energy away from the spouse and into any number of other things – political activism, children, growing her own business, charity work. The Pilgrim's love, the need for strong engagement with something, will find a goal. It has to.

The Pilgrim is the one who explores this, but it's the Warrior who has to stand up and change things. Notice, the Warrior doesn't have to fight those who don't see who she really is. The Warrior simply has to *love* her authentic inner self, validating it, and using that second part of herself to become a full Warrior-Lover.

When we accept ourselves, without judgments, we cannot help but love what we see. We also find that, in accepting ourselves, we open our hearts to accepting and loving others. They, in their turn, find it much easier to accept us.

In group work and workshops I see a version of this all the time. I've noticed that when people talk honestly and without pretence about their lives, everyone in the room is offered a chance to become more real. They almost always take that opportunity. It's as if they've been waiting for it all their lives. And some of them have. For when a person relaxes all roles, all desire to entertain or please or impress, when that person can simply be and speak his or her truth, then it is almost impossible not to feel love for that person.

At that point it doesn't matter what anyone's age is, what they do for a living, how much they earn. None of it matters, because we love the core of the person. Sometimes that allows us to love ourselves more, when we see that we are, in our centers, acceptable and loveable.

The Pilgrim has begun to see this; the Warrior-Lover acts on it.

Occasionally this can be dangerous. Timothy Treadwell, a man who spent thirteen years walking in the wild with grizzly bears, described himself as an "Animal Warrior," protecting these dangerous creatures and their habitat. "I will die for these animals," he declared, and unfortunately he did; he was killed by one of "his" bears. Whether we consider him to be a saint, a lunatic, or a weirdo matters less than that he found something he was prepared to love and to fight (peacefully) for. That his love killed him is not the point; he did what he did regardless of the consequences. That's love and it's a sentiment worthy of Romeo.

When we act on this information, this insight, this sense that we have discovered the core of who we are and what we must do, we choose freedom. Most of us don't have to take on such a dramatic cause as Timothy Treadwell's however. Boiled down to its absolute essentials what the Warrior-Lover has to do is value her own sense of free will.

As Miguel Ruiz put it in *The Voice of Knowledge,* if we really had free will, do you think we'd choose drama, conflict, difficulty, arguments, doubt, guilt, and so on? Would we really choose misery? These actions demonstrate that most of us do *not* have free will. We're only angry, agitated, depressed and tortured because we choose to be, not knowing we have any other options. And so we can become slaves to a mindset learned from others. Remember all those people who told you that you weren't good enough, smart enough, clever enough? I'm sure you do. Those words have been haunting you ever since, in dark moments. Now, think of all those young women today who are striving to look like super-models, starving themselves in the process; and young men chewing steroids are no different. These are people who are not choosing free will.

The Warrior-Lover rejects that view in favor of loving herself, and in so doing lives from a place of personal integrity, a place of real happiness.

This is important. How can we love another successfully if we don't love ourselves? If we routinely treat ourselves poorly, isn't that how we're going to treat our loved ones? A woman put it this way in one of my workshops: "If a man doesn't present himself well, he's saying he doesn't care much about himself. I have no time for men like that. If he doesn't treat himself decently then how's he going to treat me?"

The Warrior-Lover knows that the struggle is not just an exterior fight against enemies, but an interior struggle to embrace love. For, as the Bible informs us, we must love our neighbor because he is exactly as we are, and we must love him as we love ourselves. That doesn't mean we should treat him the way we routinely treat ourselves, with all those internal negatives about how we're not good enough. It means we have to love ourselves fully and also love others the same way.

When we do that we're making the translation to the realm of the Monarch.

The true Monarch – God's Deputy according to Renaissance ideals—is the person who can see past the thin screen of ordinary pretenses, and perceive the true motives in the hearts of others. This can only come about if the Monarch truly loves and values himself. Love doesn't blind us, not at this level. It opens our eyes fully, and in order to act on love one needs to have real courage.

As we have seen, it is at Pilgrim stage that the individual begins to use courage and explore what love might be. To an outside observer this can be bewildering, for a Pilgrim can be many things sexually: she can be celibate – until she feels ready to commit as a Warrior-Lover; she can also be passionately insistent, ardent, even overwhelming. In this instance what we see is the Pilgrim's longing, the desire for *this* lover to be the real one. In this we may also see the outlines of a neediness that can mask the Pilgrim's descent back into Orphan stage. For the Orphan is the one who needs a significant other to be a certain way, who looks to the relationship to provide meaning in her life, to save her soul. Similarly we can see that the emerging Pilgrim wants a loving relationship that will move her forward, and yet she may not fully realize that no one else can do the internal psychic work for her. Our age is mercifully liberal about sexual matters, yet men and women who may in fact be looking for real love are still very often labeled as 'sluts' or 'players' when they have simply not yet moved successfully through this stage. Labels of this sort are almost always the gift of Orphans, who are trying to shield themselves from the results of their own timidity. It's not so much what one does that matters, it's the spirit in which one does it.

The Warrior-Lover is easily distinguished because she has had to learn to love and respect herself and for that reason knows how to love others fully. The restlessness of the Pilgrim has been resolved in a passionate, loving attachment. What makes these two figures so different is that the Warrior-Lover has to meet her own limitations, her own despair, and move beyond it. William Faulkner puts it like this: "All of us failed to meet our dreams of perfection. So I rate us on the basis of our splendid failure to do the impossible."

If one tries to do the impossible, as Faulkner says, then failure is pretty much guaranteed. But that does not mean the attempt was not worth while. Success is not the measure of the Warrior-Lover's achievement, since that is a measure used only by Orphans, who can agree what such a word means to them even if it is meaningless to the other archetypes.

The Warrior-Lover is not a contradiction but a balancing of opposites. This is a person who can truly be herself. And when we are ourselves we give and receive love, because we can see the core of who others are capable of being, rather than judging them for what they are not.

For the Monarch we must consider not just the example of earthly kings and queens – usually a worldly, confused, proud bunch of isolationists – but something other. Think instead of the conductor of an orchestra. The conductor does not create the music, obviously, but without her ability to get everyone working together there won't be a concert. This takes love, because all members of an orchestra are necessary and have to be cherished, and it also takes courage to say that things are going to happen a certain way.

Let's look further into that comparison and put the Monarch before us in the form of the music star, or even the celebrity filmmaker. When that figure is doing the thing for which she is famous – making music, or film – it is not a solitary process. It requires a great deal of help from others involved in the business of getting the equipment set up, managing the technical and production details and helping the artist's vision to appear. These helpers often have to be extremely inventive and creative too. Anyone who's ever been in a musical ensemble knows that a performance is very often about all the people concerned "playing" with creativity. "Let's try it this way" and "Can you do that again – that was good!" These are the sounds of creative collaboration.

And when the creation is genuine it touches souls, moves us to joy or tears, and it is so much more than just one star performer's gig.

Sometimes it's so very much greater that the performers themselves can't quite work out how it all came together in this magical way, where the audience members are no longer passive spectators but active contributors to the emotions. This is when the Monarch becomes a Magician.

The Magician is the one who can make this happen without giving orders or making demands. The Magician stimulates, allows, and fosters the creativity of everyone concerned. Jesus couldn't have done what he did without his disciples and even his least obviously successful gig – the Crucifixion – turned out to be the most astoundingly creative, moving, and far-reaching action. It was that disastrous day at Golgotha that led directly to the twelve disciples going out on their own to spread the word. That stark and horrible event energized them. Seeming disasters can be magnificent triumphs when the Magician is at work.

If we take this to a more everyday level, I have a teacher colleague who puts it this way, "When I was younger I learned how to wow my classes. As I grew older I discovered it was much more important for them to wow themselves as a result of what happened in my classes." If we hand back power and agency to those who can grow as a result, we love others more than we love the ego-gratification of being seen to do a good job. It's a much higher love. It also takes a courage which is much closer to faith than anything else.

The Magician therefore is a lover in the very highest sense who promotes the creative, generative love that makes the world a better place. If people around us are happy, loving, and creative, we are all happier. At this point there is no real difference between love and creativity. Artists paint because they are in love with the visions they perceive. Writers write in cold garrets because they are in love with what they have to say about their sense of things. And so on. Art and creativity are both ultimately about a true, profound love.

There is hate-filled work out there, of course, but it's not Art. It's propaganda and it demands we see things only one way. Real Art doesn't seek to confine us; it seeks to open up discussions. That's why no two people can agree precisely on the "meaning" of a work; each will see it slightly differently, personally. And this is as it should be: freedom allows freedom, and in that freedom we find ourselves.

When artists create and share their art they change our mood, our mindset. Who hasn't gone to a concert and come away in a different mood? That's why we go; beautiful music changes us. We come out feeling better, greater than when we went in. All that has happened is we've heard a bunch of sounds, but those sounds have lifted us up and actually changed our body-chemistry, because every emotion is linked to a change in our hormone levels and our brain chemistry. That's Magic. No wonder the legend of Orpheus, the gifted lyre-player, is so powerful: Orpheus could tame wild animals, even rocks moved under his spell. The ancient Greeks knew metaphor well – change your mood and you can move formerly insurmountable objects. This is the transformative power of music and of any art. We come away from a concert, a gallery, a book, seeing the world around us in a new way. People can also achieve that just by talking with each other. There are those people in whose presence we become more alert, more intelligent, and more honest. People who have suffered and who know about personal regeneration can have an unusual magnetism for us. Music performers, who sing out their truths, loud and unashamedly, sometimes don't even need good voices; for instance, Dylan, Leonard Cohen and others do not have stellar voices. And what we see is that people move towards them. The performer comes on stage and everyone wants to get closer. Why? Could it be because that strange magnetism that comes from someone who we know can change our energy actually pulls us to him or her? Or is it that, deep down inside, we recognize the transformative power of the Magician and we long to get closer to it?

As we know, a person can be a Magician on stage and a thoroughly nasty piece of work in private life. This is the person who is able to be a Magician only when working the spell, only for that moment – and then cannot go quietly back to being a responsible Monarch. Indeed, the Magician's power can be so intoxicating that the figure stops thinking the normal rules of responsibility apply to him.

The Magician must always remember, therefore, where that creativity comes from – it comes from God, or Spirit, or whatever name you have for the power that created our universe, and is on loan to each of us.

Perhaps *A Course in Miracles* says it best in Chapter 3:

> The Holy Spirit teaches you to awaken others. As you see them waken you will learn what waking means, and because you chose to wake them their gratitude and appreciation of what you have given them will teach you its value.

This is certainly what the Monarch has to learn and the Magician has to practice, even though we can all get glimpses of this at any stage. Any one who has ever tried it will vouch for the cliché of "the best way to learn something is to try teaching it." Writers sometimes have reported to me that on re-reading their own words they've been astounded by what they allowed themselves to know on the page, but didn't fully know that they knew. In my workshops and classes I use writing to help people get to exactly this place. Sometimes I've even had to say to my students: 'Re-read your words. You're wiser than you know. Take your own excellent advice.' Occasionally I've had writers read their works to a group only to stop, stunned, and ask, 'Why do I live like I do when I know *this*?'

In my own work I've had the same unnerving experience. A novel I wrote (that remains unpublished) spelled out the theory of archetypes that became my book *Stories We Need to Know* long before I had ever consciously articulated the ideas. I knew more than I knew. Later, when I had the theory mapped out and I began to teach it I got a glimpse of what *A Course in Miracles* was telling me. And when I read those words I said: "Of course! That's why I teach!" The insights I seek to convey become far more powerful than they originally were when they're reflected back from others, and they teach me the value of what has been trying to get itself communicated through me. Any parent who has gazed at her child in wonder, witnessing the child's excitement in learning, knows what this is all about. At times like that we see with new eyes, through the child's eyes, and what a gift that can be!

This is the realm of the Magician in every part of his or her life. The task is to nurture the conditions under which others can attain, if only briefly, Magician stage. An example of this could be seen, perhaps, in the actions of Renaissance rulers, many of whom attracted and nurtured some of the finest artists of the time. The roof of the Sistine Chapel would not have been painted if Pope Julius II hadn't forced Michelangelo to paint it. Of course, Julius may have been working to ensure his own glory, but at that point in his thinking he knew beyond any doubt he would be commissioning an outstanding masterpiece, one that would inspire and uplift all who saw it. And it does still. Julius certainly had the political savvy and ruthless energy that made him a rather ferocious Monarch, yet he also could allow that part of himself to be balanced by the compassion that is necessary for the appreciation of real art. When he was alert to that impulse he became the Magician who allowed other Magicians to flourish.

This brings us to the next consideration, which is that if the highest calling of the Monarch is to be seen as creativity and the nurturing of it, we have also to remember that creativity's first guiding force is love. When a musician is moved to create music it is usually in response to some emotion about what it feels like to be in the world of sounds. The artist is celebrating something to do with life. The painter sees color or form or movement and wishes to use that experience. In doing so the creative spirit honors an aspect of the perceived world. Each created deed, each creative act, Has the capability of being a love offering to the world. Creativity is love, and it is also a communication about love.

Points to Ponder

If you have read and agreed with these pages, you'll see there may be some reasons for the premise with which we started, that human beings are on this earth in order to learn lessons about love. These lessons also include parallel lessons about courage and creativity. The main thrust of the six developmental stages as they are described here is to suggest that we are on earth to discover this highest level of love, respond to it, and ultimately to communicate it to others. The Dalai Lama sees things similarly when he writes in *The Art of Happiness* that the aim of humankind is to be happy, no matter what, and to show it. We are here to communicate to each other the majesty of existence, no matter how many small or large annoyances there are in our lives.

Obviously, reaching the same level as the Dalai Lama isn't an easy task. That's not the point. The point seems to be that all of us can experience sublime moments *at times*. Whether this comes to you from meditation, or from reading a beautiful poem, painting a wonderful picture, or seeing a magnificent sunrise – the precise method doesn't matter. It's a glimpse of what could be, of the perfection that is always with us in the present if we choose to see it. And when we get there we have become Magicians. And here is the central issue: these moments are available to all of us, no matter where we are in our lives, in flashes. Our task is to realize that these flashes are not just isolated, but they can be promises of something larger. Like a mountain top that is glimpsed from time to time when we walk through a forest, the fact that we can't see it all the time does not mean the mountain has ceased to exist when we lose sight of it. It's there, we just have to try and get closer to it so we can see more of it more of the time. Only God is at this level of awareness all the time, I suppose. The rest of us have moments, flashes of this experience, and we can get closer to this state if we remember we are here to experience and to give love, so it can grow.

Love does, truly, work miracles. People become far more than they thought they could be when they are moved by real love. We call it "heart" when we see our favorite team win, perhaps. Yet working together in absolute trust and devotion to their cause, the successful team is all about love. It may be "love of the game," but that's really not that different from love of a noble cause – it differs only in degree. The athlete who gives her all in a game is only a few steps away from the total giving of the saint who devotes a lifetime to a cause. If you can do it for a few minutes you can practice and do it for a lifetime. The primary force in use in each case is the same.

We are here to create more loving-kindness on the earth: that is when the Magic will occur.

Love of this sort does not perceive error, it only accepts good.

What does this mean? When you are driving and take a wrong turn you may find yourself spending some anxious moments before you find the correct road again. When you do, you can choose to be contented that you are on course or you can choose to beat yourself up for making a mistake. But if you do berate yourself, you will poison all the pleasure of being on the right path. Only unhappy people reproach each other or themselves for their past errors. The best way forward is not to allow the error to be important. There's a version of this in the Bible, in the Prodigal Son parable, in which the wasteful son returns home destitute. It really doesn't matter what the erring son did when he was being silly, drinking and gambling away his inheritance. What matters is he's sorry and he's come back home hoping to start over. In the parable his older brother doesn't get it: why should he celebrate someone who has made a series of poor choices? The father doesn't spend much time trying to explain; it's hard to explain anything to those who insist on living with the memory of past injuries every day. The brother may have been dutiful and loyal, where the Prodigal Son had not been, but he has just revealed himself as judgmental and unforgiving and he wants to punish, not to love. He wants to be right more than he wants to celebrate the return of someone he thought was dead – his own brother!

Imagine how this could change our world. Imagine if we chose to let go of needing to be proved right all the time. Imagine what things could be like if we didn't want to point out how correct we've been all along, or if we let go of telling others how badly they've messed up, or if we stopped blaming our past, our parents, our upbringing, or our ex-spouse for our situation. Imagine if we just stopped doing that. And then think of how things could be if entire nations and religious groups would do the same thing – if they stopped insisting that their way was the only way. Recriminations would have no value and we'd look past them to the loving soul that is each person. We'd accept others with our hearts, rather than judging them with our egos. We can choose happiness and we can choose love, any time we want.

In terms of the overlap between love and creativity we have to recognize it's not just about ourselves. That means we have to love and honor the creativity in our families – our spouses, our parents, our children – even if it seems bizarre to us. We must respect the creative devotion of the stock-broker (who makes many thoughtful decisions each day) even if it is not obviously the same as the sculptor's process. And we must do this for all our family members.

Where families seem so often to go wrong is that they don't accept their members' creative urges. The child who loves animated cartoons may well be on the way to an artistic vision of his own, or perhaps he's just going through a phase, so ordering him to stop looking at them will breed resentments. It may even undermine his own sense of creativity, and leave him, in his late teens, dismissive of anything creative, or even unable to mobilize his own generative forces.

My own example was that as a young child I was always told exactly what to wear by my mother. Then from age eight I was sent to schools that required uniforms, and later on there were even specific required "casual" clothes for those of us who were boarders. I didn't get to pick most of my clothes until I was 18. And when I did finally have some money and could choose for myself, I had almost no idea what to buy. I was out of practice. Meanwhile the girls in my neighborhood had all been choosing their clothes since shortly after they got out of diapers and so had developed their own sense of style, and of what worked for them. They had no trouble selecting colors and styles. Me, I went for jeans and dark sweaters as a way to avoid making mistakes. I was a clothing Orphan, just trying to fit in. Well, it didn't do me any lasting damage, but I use it as a simple example. It's just an instance of one way that creativity can be squashed.

Does it seem trivial? Let's take this example beyond the personal. Think about it this way: dressing nicely is about self esteem, surely, and it's about loving the things the world has to offer, and respecting our right to enjoy them. When we dress reasonably we respect ourselves at a most basic level because it reflects the love we feel for the body we inhabit. Being at peace in our own bodies, loving who we are while being perfectly aware of our faults – well, that's not as common as one might think. As anorexia and bulimia show no signs of dying out, as cosmetics manufacturers and cosmetic surgeons grow wealthier, and as America becomes the most obese nation in the world, we have a right, I think, to ask how comfortable we are in our skins, and what that says about us. We are not presently in a loving culture and we do not love ourselves.

In terms of the ambivalent relationship Americans have to body image, and the resultant self-loathing, we could pursue this even further. Manufacturers, who know that the food is not good for us, market the junk food that is routinely blamed for the epidemic of obesity in this country. What they care about is that it sells and it makes money. If they were acting in a truly loving way, would they stuff all that extra sugar and salt and trans-fat into the food? I don't think so. Do you think they insist that their own children eat those products? I doubt it. The manufacturers are not acting in a loving way and the people who buy this kind of food know that they do not really love themselves when they consume it. It's convenient, fast, and seems cheap at the time – although it isn't. A truly loving attitude on behalf of seller and consumer would actively question what is going on. It would never be enough just to say 'I like it' and to scarf down another burger. Instead we'd love ourselves enough to ask what it is we're eating. But Orphans don't question; they accept what they're offered because at heart they don't truly believe they are lovable and they don't believe they deserve food that is wholesome. So even eating becomes a way of diminishing their sense of self-esteem.

Over the decades many devoted people have fought hard for the right to have food that is not laced with poisons and carcinogens. That is not just self-love but reflects the thoughtful, reasoned love of the Warrior-Lover who is prepared to take a stand for herself, her children, and everyone. From arsenic and lead in water to alum contamination designed to make white bread whiter, to hormones and antibiotics in meat and milk – these are struggles that are worth undertaking, and they are loving struggles.

Taking what you are given, even when we know it's not good, is a way of saying that we don't believe we deserve good treatment, that we don't deserve love. When we stop loving ourselves in this way, real courage begins to fade and die.

Love, you see, is an issue that pervades every part of our lives.

And this brings us back to a point I made earlier, but which bears repeating. The Magician's gift is to remind us that we are all linked to the almost limitless creativity of our world. We are all linked whether we wish to be or not. The Magician knows there is no separation between people except whatever it is we create to stoke up our egos and make ourselves feel better. We are living an example of that right now, as you are reading this book. It was written by someone (me) who was born in England in a location that may be very far from what you call home. These words appear before you on paper that was milled from trees grown in Canada, or Siberia, or Northfield, Massachusetts; trees that were cut down by Native Americans, Cambodians, Kosovar exiles, second-generation Hispanics or seventh generation Irish, using Chinese-made chain saws assembled in New Jersey and fuelled with gasoline blended from eight different countries. We are linked to far more than we care to recognize on a daily basis, only we choose not to see that. The ego insists on telling us that we need not bother to look at that; but if we do acknowledge it and put aside our ego myopia, then we will probably find ourselves feeling very grateful for all we have and for the complex web of interlinked lives that makes it happen. Gratitude is love, also.

Love, courage, honesty, and creativity: without love no courage can appear, and without courage there will be no honesty, and certainly no real creativity. Remember the centuries old Christian triad that used to be Faith, Hope and Charity? This has now been altered (as we saw) to Faith, Hope, and Love. Love is in fact the bedrock of Faith and Hope, which in turn are the basis of everything else that is good. It takes Love for us to have Hope. Hope is the expectation that the world one inhabits is truly worthy of being trusted. Faith is that same confidence projected into the future. Love in its most developed form is the foundation of all this. Our task, and the message on these pages, has been to point out that love exists on many different levels and that we do ourselves no favors if we insist on seeing only one aspect of it, for as we grow in awareness love redefines itself in front of our eyes. We know this just as we all know that our teenage crushes were not as important as they seemed at the time – although when we were caught up in the thick of those experiences they seemed to be the biggest thing in our world. We grew up, gradually, and love needed to be reassessed as we became wiser.

If we don't know there is a higher, deeper, finer, stronger version of love then we are more than likely to settle for whatever is on offer, and never seek for more. The six archetypes tell us that there is more to know about love, and that it is worth making the effort to do so.

At the highest level, the Magician loves the creative force of the universe, God, whatever one wishes to call it, so completely that she becomes a conduit for that energy, and when that happens miracles occur. At those moments people are healed of diseases they've had for years, or shed acute conditions that were supposed to be fatal, or they see with new eyes and turn their lives around.

The greatest lesson any of us ever has to learn is the lesson of love, and it may just be that it's the only lesson there is.

Notes

1. Timothy Treadwell was the subject of several PBS documentaries and also of Werner Herzog's film *Grizzly Man*, Lion's Gate Films, 2005. In each case film-makers used Treadwell's own remarkable film footage to some degree.
2. Miguel Ruiz, and Janet Mills, *The Voice of Knowledge: A Practical Guide to Inner Peace* (San Rafael, CA: Amber-Allen Publishers, 2004).
3. William Faulkner quotation is from www.littlebluelight.com.
4. *A Course in Miracles*, op.cit. p.174.
5. His Holiness the Dalai Lama *The Art of Happiness: A Handbook for Living* (New York: Riverhead, 1998).
6. The parable of the Prodigal Son appears in Luke 15: 11-32.

Chapter Eleven

The Six Stages of Love in Fairy Tales, Folk Tales, and Modern Times

ॐ

———————————— _◦ ◦_ ————————————

To close this discussion of love and the archetypes in our culture, I'd like to give some specific examples that show the way that archetypes can work as part of an active narrative – in each case a highly popular narrative treasured over generations. I've chosen to look at two old German folk tales collected by the Grimm brothers and at a modern 'classic' movie, *Casablanca*, because they share some remarkable similarities. For in each case they are about how the main figures can progress through the six archetypes, moving towards love, and also about how anyone can become stuck along the way.

Before we can proceed, though, we'll need to take a moment to consider how folk tales work, so that we can appreciate their power fully. Like the Tarot, the folk tale is a way to depict the archetypal stages in a memorable form: both work on the human imagination in a specific way, forming pictures for us to become attached to, and these archetypal images are first and foremost a visual form. We construct those images in our minds in response to stories we have heard or as a direct result of seeing the images on pages or cards. Perhaps we have only to look at the way children connect with fairy tales in order to understand the quality for infiltrating our memories and our thinking that these archetypes clearly possess. Children love to have fairy tales read to them from a book, long before they can read for themselves, and they love to gaze at the illustrations. They protest any attempt to alter or shorten the stories (as weary adults will know from experience). The child will grow up and may forget many things – but not Cinderella or Snow White. The images have a remarkable tendency to stick, and the memory does not hold onto anything unless it feels vital. Daniel Schacter in *The Seven Sins of Memory* has demonstrated that we remember what feels rich and important, and we discard the rest. That is perhaps why we can recall some folk tales and some stories all our lives while others, read just as frequently under exactly similar circumstances, fade forever.

In the not so distant past folk tales and fairy stories were powerful for those who heard them because they were repeated (often by a stranger who was an itinerant story teller and therefore a figure of some mystery) and the repetitions most likely occurred at night, gathered around the fireside. As anyone who ever went to camp as a kid knows, those stories told around the fire have a power that they would never have if repeated in broad daylight. Mystery and repetition were the keys, and these tales had, potentially, great persuasive power.

Not all folk tales are first rate, of course. Some are mere moral fables. Others have trick endings designed to raise a laugh. Yet there are other examples that seem to radiate a deeper meaning, and these tend to be longer and of a more subtle texture than others; these are the myths that we sense contain important psychological truths. It's hard to describe, but even a casual reading of a collection of folk tales will yield many that are totally forgettable, and a few which are absolutely haunting.

One thing that needs to be made clear is that these mythic folk tales were remembered and repeated with scrupulous accuracy by their tellers. As Joseph Campbell put it, 'Myths and legends may furnish entertainment incidentally, but they are essentially tutorial.' As teaching tools they had to remain accurate in their essential components.

Grimm makes this point absolutely plain in his commentary on his rendition of the stories. He states that these particular tales were not mutilated by random improvisations at the whim of the teller. Indeed, there certainly were variations, but the central elements of the stories, the overall structures, remained intact. Grimm wrote them down because he feared that as times changed they would be distorted or lost, but until he took on this task no one had set about recording them in anything but a haphazard manner. They existed only in the memories of those who knew and loved them. It is the accuracy of their transmission that makes these tales very much like the Tarot deck: there are many stylistic variants of the deck but the specific elements of each card are repeated precisely down the centuries, for it is in those details that the significance of the card is conveyed. It's clear that we're dealing with a system that in both cases values specifics because they are seen to reflect larger truths. We could shrug this off by saying that bygone eras were more conservative and so maintained traditional patterns as a matter of course, but that would be both patronizing and unintelligent. Since the year 1200 (the approximate date of the rapid growth of written literature and also of the appearance of the Tarot) names, spellings, speech patterns, and grammar have all varied enormously in every European language. We would today have great trouble understanding spoken or written English as it was 800 years ago. Yet our language has been subject to exactly the same forces as both folk tales and archetypal representations in stories. The language has varied; the structures of folk tales have remained constant. These tales and images have endured in exactly the same ways as geographical features of the landscape remain intact, because they are the basic patterns against which daily life carries on.

The two folk tales I wish to address here, and which particularly stand out in the Grimm Brothers' collection, are called *The Gold-Children* and *The Brothers*. They are clearly variants on a similar theme and have substantial structural elements in common. Max Luthi links these two tales to a whole class of stories, all of which have the same elements, and which he groups as 'dragon slayer' tales. The basic plot for each is as follows: in both tales twin brothers leave home with their adopted animals to look for good fortune in the world, until one brother turns back, discouraged; the other continues. When they part in *The Brothers* they drive a knife into a tree, one side of the blade facing the direction each will take, and they agree that if the blade rusts that this will mean the brother who went in that direction needs help. In *The Gold-Children* the same idea applies but the object is a pair of gold lilies, one for each brother, which will wilt if either is in difficulties. In both tales the twin who continues faces a challenge and finds a maiden to marry. In one instance he has to kill a dragon and is, temporarily, cheated of his prize by the king's Marshall. When marriage is achieved, the brother in each case decides to go hunting – despite his wife's pleas not to. While out in the woods he meets a witch who turns him to stone. He remains a statue until the brother who had returned home sees the knife blade rust (or the lily wilt) and sets off to rescue him. The witch is forced to reverse her magic, whereupon the brother is brought back to life, returns home to his wife, and is happy for ever after.

What is remarkable about these two tales is that they each focus on just one of the twin brothers. In both tales, the twins leave home with their adopted animal followers (a mirroring of the Orphan phase) and take to the road; at a certain point they part. In the first tale, one brother returns home after experiencing the rejections of the wider world, choosing to return to his Innocent self, while in the other story, the twin just wanders about looking for work. In *The Gold-Children* the wandering brother has to disguise himself in a bear skin to avoid robbers who might be attracted by the gold of his skin, which suggests the way the emerging Pilgrim has to concentrate on nurturing his inner worth rather than worrying about outer show. It is the gold within that matters. He then finds a maiden to wed who loves him despite his outer raggedness. He is in this instance a Pilgrim, determined to go ahead no matter that even his brother has other ideas, and he finds someone who will love his interior qualities, and risk parental wrath for him, so he has found himself as a Warrior-Lover. In the other tale the brother takes on a fight with a dragon, and he is more easily identifiable as a Warrior-Lover.

Now, before we can continue with the tales we must make some observations. One point to pay attention to (which occurs in a large number of other tales in which the central figure takes to the road) is that in each case the main character takes something along with him from his home, whether it be the adopted animals or his golden skin and golden horse, or in some versions it is simply the tools of his trade. It's a small detail but potent, since it reflects a psychological truth. When we become Orphans we want someone to take care of us, but when we become Pilgrims we must learn how to use our past experiences and abilities, the things we carry with us, as tools to help ourselves. In many folk tales this involves using what the main character is carrying generously to help others, which then gives rise to a better reward later. For instance, in *Donkey Cabbages*, another folk tale in the Grimm collection, the wandering huntsman gives money to the old lady who then tells him how to use his gun to shoot the bird that will provide him with the wishing-cloak and whose heart, once swallowed, will ensure he finds a gold coin under his pillow each morning. It's a familiar formula in many tales. In psychic terms it tells us not to cling blindly to the hopes that come with money, but to exercise spiritual generosity and openness, to respect others, and to listen to what they may tell us about how we can use our skills. In fact we have to be willing to take chances and be open to possibilities, which is what the Pilgrim has to be aware of. The Orphan mentality would be to hold on to money when it's in short supply and not give it away. The Pilgrim, however, cannot truly become a Pilgrim in these tales until he acts generously and with openness. When he does this he finds he gains more tools that then propel him on to the challenges he will face; without those tools he could not have thought about any sort of quest at all.

It's an important point about the transition from Orphan to Pilgrim. Put in modern terms, we all have preconceptions and emotional baggage. The vital thing is not to hold on to these, but to use them. I've observed many students who had poor grade school experiences, who came to college determined to graduate with a degree in education, and who dedicated themselves to becoming better teachers than those who hurt them. That's an example of taking what you have and using it differently, productively, and where hurt is changed to healing and love rather than resentment. In symbolic terms, listening to the 'old woman' or the dwarf, or whichever figure appears, can be seen as being open to ideas that come from others, no matter how odd they may be, and it can also represent the need to listen to one's own sense of inner wisdom. This is what will start us on our Pilgrim quest, when we release ourselves from conventional thinking.

Returning to *The Brothers* and *The Gold-Children*, in both stories the venturesome brother marries despite the opposition of the parent or authority figure and he becomes a Warrior-Lover in the domestic arena. For example, in *The Brothers* the twin gains the love of the princess because he kills a huge dragon, although the

King's Marshall then cheats him out of his reward for a year. After he has exposed the Marshall he marries the Princess and is greeted as a Prince by his new father-in-law. In *The Gold-Children* the marriage is allowed after the father of the bride sees the young man's golden skin and decides not to have him killed. In both cases the young men have shown their inner worth. For some folk tales this would be a natural ending point, but both of these tales continue, deepening the value of what they have to convey.

In both stories the married twin chases off on a quest (after a stag or a hind), meets a witch and is turned to stone. At this point the other twin sees the flower wilt, or the knife blade rust, immediately recognizes what it means, and comes to the rescue, freeing the enchanted twin and bringing him back to his wife.

In archetypal terms this indicates that the Warrior-Lover can become stuck as he makes his way to Monarch level, choosing to run around fruitlessly rather than to grow in wisdom. Hunting the stag was traditionally the purview of the Monarch only, so we could take this to mean that when one is happily joined to another as a lover there is a temptation to act like a Monarch even though one isn't, yet. To some extent this mirrors the idea we discussed earlier about the danger for the Warrior-Lover of indulging in an exclusive relationship, which can divert anyone from a wider sense of who he or she could be. In *The Brothers* the wife pleads with the twin not to go hunting. The fact that he disregards her pleas shows he's not in full harmony with her, not ready yet to be in a balanced Monarch pairing. He decides to overrule her and please himself. Since the Monarch has to be a complete balance of the masculine and the feminine aspects of the self, this is a way in which the tales suggest just how love can go wrong.

The brother rides out, meets the witch and is turned to stone because he acts imperiously towards her (he threatens to shoot her yapping dog). The variation on this in *The Brothers* is that the young man agrees to strike his own animals with a wand to make them harmless. In doing this he offends against the instinctual, intuitive loyalty of the animal realm and fails to respect those creatures that have been so supportive to him. The twinned animals, we'll recall, were the ones who rushed forward and finished off the dragon when he was unable to complete the task. When he renders his animal helpers harmless he becomes defenseless against the witch. The symbolism is fairly accessible – the pseudo-Monarch becomes overbearing and disregards his faithful followers. As a result the feminine aspect of himself, which was emblematized in the bride, becomes something much less wholesome in the form of the witch who turns him to stone. It's a way of saying that the marriage has become stuck and a dead end. Today this brother would probably not be hunting a stag; he'd be playing golf obsessively, or be a workaholic. In reaction his wife would most likely become more and more discontented

– a witch in popular parlance – until the marriage really started to feel dead, unable to change in any way.

This brother has run into marital trouble because he has stopped listening to his wife, and therefore the 'feminine' part of himself, and also because he is no longer in a vital and respectful relationship to his own instinctual self, as emblematized in his disregard for the animals that have been part of his life until now. He is like an unbalanced Monarch: he disregards those who are loyal to and dependent upon him.

This is when the other brother comes to the rescue – the other part of the self. This brother is not fooled by the witch and in fact he knows exactly where to go and how to force her to reverse the spell. The first brother is revived and, no longer stuck in his role, he embraces his rescuer, who has come straight from the parental home. As such he could be seen as the Innocent who has taken on Orphan status, gone on a Pilgrimage and challenged the evil witch as a Warrior-Lover who loves his brother. Notice he does this not for gain but because of his sense of being vitally linked to his twin. In addition he is not fooled by the old witch, as he sees right away that she is trouble. His judgments have not been clouded by the ego-longings his brother responded to. And so the revived brother returns to his wife and much joy. In several variants of the tale, they then become King and Queen.

An important episode that exists midway through *The Brothers*, but not in all variants, shows how the brother who killed the dragon sends his tame animals to get food and clothing for him from the King's own store. He is determined to be as well-appointed as the King himself when he goes to claim the King's daughter. This sort of emphasis on outer show tends to reinforce the notion that this brother is misled by ego concerns about how good he seems in the eyes of others.

The theme that emerges is that the uncorrupted brother gives life to the brother who is confused and entrapped by the destructive aspect of the Shadow self. This is exactly what the Warrior-Lover and the Monarch have to face, that desire to be overpowering, right, and overly forceful, thus ignoring the feminine aspect of the self. His unblemished loving self (the twin brother) guides him back to where he needs to be.

Notice that the second brother does not threaten the witch's dog – an emblem of fidelity – because he is faithful to his brother, to his sense of the completed self. He cannot let his brother exist as a half person, stuck, frozen and helpless. He needs his twin to be whole, just as that knife blade needs both sides to be free of rust or it is weakened, and just as we all need to become whole people before we can link fully with our lovers. He reminds his twin that no one exists alone, and conducts him back to his deepest connection – his wife.

The tales are astonishingly similar to five of the six stages, and even though the Monarch Pairing is the highest level that is obviously achieved, we have to recall the words that end almost all folk tales – 'they all lived happily ever after.' That is a gesture towards the sense of fulfillment and connection to the divine that the Magician achieves. The arrival of the Innocent twin enables the evil charm to be reversed. Perhaps it is only when the Monarch can perceive the example of the Innocent's devotion that the Magician comes into being. In modern terms it is sometimes only when we see the love small children (who are Innocents) have for their parents that we begin to rethink what love might be in our own lives.

The tales are surprisingly subtle in that the choice of twins is a detail which reminds the reader that no one exists alone, unattached, and whole unto himself; that is the delusion of the ego. That's the sort of thinking that emphasizes what 'I' have achieved, rather than considering where circumstances have brought us. When the twin hunts the stag or the hind, it's not about finding food; it's about bringing home a trophy. That's the ego at work. The arrival of the second twin reminds us that we are all linked to each other; we are all part of the divine creation and when we forget that, it is as if we have cast aside half of our selfhood. If we do that, then we do indeed become about as useful and as aware as stone statues.

The tale is an elegant assessment of a central human struggle that has to do with loving one's true self as a vital part of creation, rather than loving the rewards of the ego – and it sketches out the struggles faced at each point with economy and accuracy. To some extent it is always the ego that sends us out into the world as Pilgrims, for without it we wouldn't set out at all. The task then is to find out who we are in terms that are not simply limited to the way the ego sees things.

We can always discount folk tales and say they've been hopelessly altered and botched over the years, and that is partly why I choose to offer here two tales that are substantially the same. They show how tales can be altered but still retain the essential elements we are talking about. What's remarkable about these two tales is the psychological sophistication they demonstrate. In the rural remoteness of some odd corners of Germany one might expect that notions of love and personal growth would be rudimentary. It turns out they are not. The tales have insights that can speak to us now, today. For today we have plenty of golf widows who are ignored, just as the Princess is. Husbands often seem clueless as to why their beautiful brides have become resentful witches when all the men have done is not be at home much. Like the brother who agrees to have his faithful animals turned to stone, parents ignore their families and bosses ignore their employees and board members. When things go out of balance like this they can't see where they've gone wrong. And they don't know how to save the situation. The answer, as the tales suggest, is to reconnect to that part of the Innocent that is trusting and loving and that values the reciprocity of real loving connection. It means leaving the temptations of the ego behind. It means putting love first. And then the magic appears.

Now, let's take a look at a different story, a modern work that has become a sort of folk tale of its own. I'm referring to *Casablanca*, the Bogart-Bergman legend that was first screened in 1942, directed by Michael Curtiz. In it we can see another example of how characters can get stuck when on their ways to achieving love.

The movie was not expected at the time to be any sort of box office smash hit, yet it has endured and become something of a cultural icon. It was seen at first as a tale that commented fairly overtly on the initial US policy of neutrality to the Axis forces during World War II. Yet its appeal has lingered far beyond that time and exists, in part, because it reflects aspects of spiritual development in the totality of the story that have had a deep personal resonance for many people for over sixty years.

Most of us know the plot, and even the words of *As Time Goes By* as played by Sam the pianist. The movie's central action starts when Rick, a somewhat shady American bar owner in Casablanca, is surprised by the reappearance of Ilsa, his lover when they were in Paris just as the Germans invaded in 1940. He was hurt by her desertion of him then and is still smarting. Unfortunately for him she is now with her husband, Victor, an anti-Nazi activist who is trying to leave Morocco for Lisbon and then the USA to continue his struggle. America is still officially neutral at this time (1941), and Rick makes it quite obvious that he only cares about himself. Through a twist of fate Rick is handed the documents Victor and Ilsa need in order to leave. He thinks about using the documents for his own advantage, and then decides to use them to allow the threatened Victor and Ilsa to escape. He then has to get them and the documents to the airport, outwit both the Nazis in the shape of Major Strasser, and Captain Renault, the French police chief, and convince Ilsa to leave with her husband rather than with Rick himself. It takes some effort, which drags Rick out of his neutrality, turning him once more into a man who believes in something other than making money.

In terms of archetypes the pattern is very clear. At the start of the movie Rick is an Orphan holed up in Casablanca, making various semi-legal deals with other profiteers and scoundrels. His past is shadowy, everyone deals with him, and he is known variously as Rick, Richard, Ricky, Mr. Rick, and Monsieur Blaine, which suggests that he can be anything to anyone as long as business demands it. But there is more to him than this. We discover that he has, in the past, been a gun runner to both the Ethiopians (fighting the Italian fascists) and to the Spanish republicans (fighting Franco's fascists). So, at one time, his heart was in the right place; perhaps he was even a Warrior-Lover then, but clearly he has now slipped back into the Orphan's defensive cynicism.

Ilsa now appears. When they met and fell in love in Paris she was, literally, an Orphan, believing her husband dead and not knowing where to turn. She greets Rick, now, though, as a Monarch. She loves her husband and she is devoted to his cause. She makes the mistake of trying to talk to Rick and explain herself – she didn't know her husband was still alive when she fell in love with Rick – but he's too drunk and too much in the self-pitying Orphan mind set to be able to hear what she says.

For our discussion we could say that both Ilsa and Rick have been attached to causes that have somehow let them down (if only temporarily in Ilsa's case) so they meet in Paris as defeated Warrior-Lovers who have slipped back to being Orphans. No wonder they fall in love so easily! They are exactly alike, seeking the shelter of sympathetic arms.

Rick remains the wounded Orphan until Ilsa comes back to see him a second time at his cafe, braving the curfew. She certainly demonstrates courage and when she draws a gun on him to get him to part with the papers she and Victor need, he sees something in her that he had forgotten in himself. For a while she is impressive, then she collapses into his arms saying, "I don't know what's right or wrong anymore." Effectively the strain is too much for her and she slips back into Orphan existence, wanting someone else to decide her fate. At that point Rick sees the Warrior-Lover that she can be and decides he has to step forward as well.

In all this Rick senses something that calls him to be the best person he can be. It is in his consequent double-dealing that he shows himself as the consummate manipulator for a good cause. It is this which enables him to get Victor and Ilsa to the airport, outwitting both Major Strasser and Captain Renault, and even Ilsa, who thinks she's getting on the plane with Rick. It's a masterful piece of dealing.

Rick's final speech to Ilsa is worth recalling, because he tells her that if she chooses him she'll only regret it: "Maybe not today. Maybe not tomorrow, but soon and for the rest of your life." There is real wisdom in this. Rick knows that he and Ilsa *could* rekindle their love, but only at the wounded Orphan level they had once known. He recognizes he could never become more than that if getting what he wanted involved betraying a good and noble cause (Victor's anti-fascist activity), and so there would be no possibility of true, honest growth in their love. Ilsa knows what it is to be part of a Monarch Pair with Victor, and even if that's hard work, nothing less will ever come close to that experience. Orphans, as we know, tend to take the shelter that is convenient at the moment; Warrior-Lovers (which is what Rick has become, at the very least) know better and can take a longer view. Of course Rick doesn't speak in terms of archetypes but it's clear he knows a thing or two about integrity and that their love was not at the highest level possible for each of them. It's an astonishing speech, really. He acknowledges that there are levels of love, and that he's not yet at the highest level, no matter how strong his personal need may be.

Victor Laszlo seems to function as a Monarch who is occasionally a Magician: he escapes from a concentration camp; his name is everywhere, a by-word for resistance to the fascists; he has a flair for uniting people against oppression and he is legendary for it. In one of the most famous scenes of the movie, the Nazis are in Rick's café singing fascist songs, and Victor orders the band to play *La Marseillaise*. It's worth noting that the bandleader looks for approval to Rick, *and he agrees*. The band strikes up, all the French stand up and bellow out their national anthem, and the Nazis are taught that they cannot get away with their overbearing ways without exciting a backlash. It's a marvelous and empowered moment. However, the victory is short-lived and Rick's bar is shut down – as he must have known it would be. But the greater moral point has been made: it's the action of a Magician to get people to be responsible for their deepest feelings and allegiances. Victor mobilizes self-respect and decency, and both are forms of love.

Victor is also interesting at a personal level because he knows that something happened between Ilsa and Rick, and he even asks her if she wants to say anything. He knows that people make mistakes, that they despair and slip into Orphan thinking, and he loves her anyway. He loves the best part of her, not her mistakes. He is in many ways a Magician, working for the highest possible good, risking everything, and bringing out the very best in people in the process. In fact he and Ilsa bring out the best in Rick. One could say that they function as a Monarch Pairing that also brings the Magician into existence when necessary.

At the climax of the movie Rick shoots Major Strasser, Renault gives up his role as a Vichy French collaborator in disgust, Victor and Ilsa take off on the plane, and Rick and Renault walk off to join the Free French at Brazzaville. They are an unlikely pair, but the famous line, 'This could be the start of a beautiful friendship' in fact shows them both as Warrior-Lovers. Orphans no longer, they are off to fight for a cause. In case we miss the point, we'll recall that both men have given up their shallow sexual lives – Rick has given up the French bargirl, and Renault has had to give up seducing young women who want exit visas – so they have moved beyond casual meaningless sex. Perhaps Ilsa has inspired them both. Perhaps Renault has also been inspired by Rick – who thwarts at least one of Renault's affairs out of a sense of moral outrage. It doesn't matter exactly how it happens because the way of the Magician is that inspiration grows seemingly of itself, and Victor has been around each of them enough that their ways of thinking have been changed forever.

And so we can see that the six archetypes are in this modern folk tale as well, and they are not just to do with sexual love, but with a love that is connected to a standard of moral conduct. From ancient tale to modern myth the preoccupations are the same, and we can understand each more fully when we see them as unfolding the six stages, showing how anyone can get stuck, and how it is possible to break free again.

These pages have been an attempt to show that our lives are journeys towards love that go through distinct stages, and that the price of failing to undertake this journey is that it leaves us as human beings who are only half alive, disconnected from the Divine and lost in the realms of the ego. The Tarot's imagery can show us the way forward, as can literature that is connected to myth, and folk tales can do this as well. Better still, our more modern stories can also guide us in the same ways if we look at them through this lens. Joseph Campbell called this "the *picture language* of the soul" (my emphasis) which he felt was linked directly to our dreams and the Collective Unconscious. Campbell traced the decline in this mythic way of thinking to the growth of the Enlightenment in Europe with its emphasis on rationality. Whether that's true or not – and it's a persuasive point – it's accurate to say that it's a primarily visual language that can show us the way forward. After a gap of some two and a half centuries it's time we paid more attention to it.

This brings us full circle, back to Gauguin's painting and the important questions he asked. He'd traveled half way round the world to Tahiti to try and get away from the stifling social pressures of a bourgeois Parisian life just so that he could get free enough to find answers. "Who are we? Where have we come from? Where are we going?" he asked. The answers are not written. Instead he showed them in the haunting, exquisite responses to the beauty of the human forms he painted. The figures are all ages, from the baby to the old woman waiting for death, and if we choose to we could see the six stages in the groupings he presents. In the expressions on their faces we can see, perhaps, that these Tahitians were not troubled by the questions that make up the painting's title at all. They were, for Gauguin, an island of Innocents unsullied by the modern world of ego concerns, people who already knew about love, detachment, and peace, and his paintings are devout offerings to their instinctual acceptance of the ways life unfolds. No wonder he had to run away to find them. He, the master painter, a Monarch in his skills, cramped in Paris, felt compelled to come to the island of the Innocents. He needed them just as the deadened soul of the twin who had lost his way needed his Innocent brother to rescue him. And, when the Innocent is invited back into the Monarch's world, when we do see with unclouded eyes and yet with wisdom, the Magician arises. The world becomes a miracle. In exploring his own question Gauguin seems to conclude that we are here to love and honor the magic of everyday beauty as we move through life's stages.

Notes

1. Daniel Schachter, *The Seven Sins of Memory* (Boston: Houghton Mifflin, 2002).
2. Joseph Campbell, in: *The Complete Grimm's Fairy Tales*, op. cit. The tales are described as 'tutorial' on p.841.
3. Wilhelm Grimm, preface to the second volume (1815). "Anyone believing that traditional materials are easily falsified and carelessly preserved, and hence cannot survive over a long period, should hear how close [Katherina Viehmann] always keeps to her story and how zealous she is for its accuracy." Quoted in *Grimm*, op. cit. p.833.
4. Campbell, Joseph, in *Grimm*, op. cit. "The picture language of the soul", p.864.
5. *The Gold-Children*, in *Grimm*, op. cit. Tale #85, pp. 388-393.
6. *The Brothers.* In *Grimm*, op. cit. Tale #60, pp. 290-311.
7. Max Luthi, *Once upon A Time : On the Nature of Fairy Tales,* trans. L. Chadeayne, and P. Gottwald, (Bloomington: Indiana Univ. Press, 1970), pp.47-58.
8. *Donkey Cabbages*, in *Grimm,* op. cit. Tale #122, pp. 551-557.
9. *Casablanca,* 1942, Directed by Michael Curtiz.

Bibliography

The Letters of Abelard and Heloise. Translated by Peter Abelard. London: Penguin, 1998.

Austen, Jane. *Emma.* London: Dent., 1961.

———*Pride and Prejudice.* New York: Dover, 1995.

Baker, Russell. *Growing Up.* New York: Signet, 1992.

Beowulf: A New Verse Translation. Seamus Heaney. New York: Norton, 2001.

Beuchner, Frederick. *Now and Then.* HarperSanFrancisco,1985.

Bloom, Harold. *The Western Canon.* Florida: Harcourt Brace, 1994.

Bolen, Jean Shinoda. *Goddesses in Everywoman.* New York: Harper and Row, 1985.

Bradshaw, John. *John Bradshaw on the Family: A New Way of Creating Solid Self Esteem.* HCI, revised 1990.

Brokaw, Tom. *The Greatest Generation.* New York: Random House, 1998.

Chaucer, Geoffrey. *The Complete Works.* Edited F.N. Robinson. Oxford: Oxford University Press, 1955.

A Course in Miracles. No author given. The Foundation for Inner Peace, London: Penguin, 1996.

Crane, Stephen. *The Red Badge of Courage.* (1895) widely reprinted.

Clinton, William. *Giving: How Each of Us Can Change the World.* New York: Knopf, 2007.

The Dalai Lama. *The Art of Happiness: A Handbook for Living.* New York: Riverhead, 1998.

Dass, Ram. *Be Here Now.* New Mexico, Lama Foundation, 1971.

Dunbar, William, *Dunbar, Selected Poems.* Edited Harriet Harvey-Wood. London: Routledge/Fyfield, 2003.

Eliot, George. *Daniel Deronda* (1876). London: Penguin Classics Edition, 1996.

———*Middlemarch* (1872). New York: Signet Classics Edition, 2003.

Fielding, Helen. *Bridget Jones' Diary.* London: Picador, 1998.

Goldwater, Robert. *Gauguin.* New York: Abrams, 1983.

Gray, John. *Men Are From Mars, Women Are from Venus*. New York: Harper-Collins, 1993.

Grimm, Jacob and Wilhelm. *The Complete Grimm's Fairy Tales*. Trans. Margaret Hunt, revised James Stern. New York: Random House, 1972.

Henryson, Robert. *Henryson's Poems*. Ed. Charles Elliot. Oxford: OUP, 1963.

Hornby, Nick. *About A Boy*. London: Penguin, 1998.

Jung, Carl Gustav. *Man and His Symbols*. New York: Doubleday, reprinted 1969.

Kipling, Rudyard. *Barrack Room Ballads* (1898). Reprinted New York: Dodo Press, 2005.

Kundera, Milan. *The Book of Laughter and Forgetting*. Trans. Aaron Asher, New York: Harper Perennial, 1999.

Lovelace, Richard. *Poems*. Widely republished.

Malory, Thomas. *Le Morte D'Arthur*. Trans. R. M. Lumiansky. New York: Scribners, 1982.

Morag, Hali. *The Complete Guide to Tarot Reading*. Had Hadsharon: Astrolog, 1998.

Ovid. *Metamorphoses*. Trans. Rolfe Humphries. Bloomington: Indiana Univ. Press, 1983.

Ruiz, Miguel, and Mills, Janet. *The Voice of Knowledge: A Practical Guide to Inner Peace*. Boston: Amber-Allen Publishers, 2004.

Schachter, Daniel. *The Seven Sins of Memory*. Boston: Houghton Mifflin, 2002.

Sanchez, Sonia. *Just Don't Never Give Up on Love*. *Callalloo*, Maryland: Johns Hopkins University Press, 1984, no. 20, pp. 83-85.

Shakespeare, William. *The Complete Works*. Ed. Peter Alexander. London: Collins, 1970.

Sophocles., The Complete Greek Tragedies. Ed. David Grene and Richard Lattimore. Chicago: Chicago University Press, 1991.

Tao Te Ching. Trans. Steven Mitchell, New York: HarperPerennial, 1988.

Tolle, Eckhart. *The Power of Now, A Guide to Spiritual Enlightenment*. Novato, CA: New World Library, 1999.

⸺*A New Earth: Awakening Your Life's Purpose,* New York: Plume, Penguin, 2005.

Watlington, Dennis. *Chasing America: Notes from a Rock'n'Soul Integrationist*. New York: Thomas Dunne Books, 2004.